The Pig and Me

The Pig and Me

Tired of hearing "you can't", one woman sets out with a pan of brownies and a skinny, pink pig to prove that she can.

Lindsay Frucci

Square Hill
2011

ISBN: 0615428223

ISBN-13: 9780615428222

Dedication

This book is dedicated, with deepest gratitude to

Bob Fox and Jay Albert - Without your belief in me and my abilities, your honest, unfailing support and your love there would be no story to tell.

Stuart Pompian - You jumped in with enthusiasm and then hung on with patience and an unwavering sense of humor. I am so glad you did.

Sallie Bowling - The woman who rescued me and kept me laughing.

And Steve Mintz - You came in at the end, guided me in the right direction and taught me that "It is what it is" and "Tomorrow is another day" aren't just words, but words to live by.

You are all special people and treasured friends.
I am blessed.

Leap, and the net will appear.

—John Burroughs

Preface

We had three cars, two sons, a golden retriever, and an in-ground pool. For seven years, my husband and I had been living the dream in a center-entrance colonial with attached two-car garage in a suburb west of Boston. Paul commuted to his job as Vice President of Sales for a software company and I was a happy stay-at-home Mom.

Now, two close friends were moving to New Hampshire to embark on a real-estate development project and wanted Paul to ditch his high-stress, high-travel corporate job and become their partner. I thought it was a wonderful idea. For weeks I'd been putting a full-court press on my reluctant husband to make the move. I was envisioning a Currier & Ives life in beautiful New Hampshire, raising two boys who would each become a combination of Huckleberry Finn and Opie from the *Andy Griffith Show.*

"I'm terrified we're going to lose everything," Paul said one night. We were making progress; a couple of weeks before, he was saying, "No way in hell."

"We won't," I replied with all the certainty that accompanies insane naiveté. "We can do this."

Paul finally caved and on a rainy spring day in 1987, we loaded a truck with the contents of our subdivision colonial and then unloaded it into a 200-year-old cape on seventeen acres.

Three years later, we handed the keys to the bank and filed for bankruptcy. My husband's worst fears had come true. We had lost everything.

Chapter 1

Sitting on the crooked stone step outside the kitchen door, I closed my eyes and let the warmth of the early summer morning wash over me. A furry golden head lay heavily on one bare foot; Rozzi's soft snore mingled with birdsong, creating a soothing harmony.

The abrupt roar of a chain saw jolted me out of my reverie. Both dogs raised their heads briefly at the familiar sound, then went back to sleep.

So much for peace and quiet.

I stood and looked beyond the yard to the small field that lay on the other side of our narrow dirt road. Several tall, limbless trees lay in the field, scattered like Lincoln Logs on a green carpet. Sawdust flew as Paul's chain saw dug into a thick trunk.

I turned and headed into the house.

"A.J.," I called to our youngest son, "we have to be out of here in fifteen minutes if I'm going to take you to Zach's before I go to work."

Four years after we filed for bankruptcy, a series of fiscally frugal steps had brought us to another old farmhouse in another small, New Hampshire town. Paul had returned to the corporate world and was gone Monday through Friday. I was selling real estate.

Our lives were dictated by what things cost. There were no restaurants and no fun family getaways. Shopping was limited to necessities. To avoid paying for pre-split firewood for our woodstove and two fireplaces, Paul was spending his two days at home each week splitting wood. I wondered how much of this time-consuming task was really about money. Or was the manual labor just a good excuse to be alone?

I walked into the living room. "Adam, honey, what are you doing today?"

My oldest was smart enough to put his video game controller down. He looked up at me with black-brown eyes fringed by thick eyelashes.

His father's eyes.

"Dunno," he answered. "How long are you gonna be gone?"

"Not sure. I'm showing three houses, so probably early afternoon."

"Oh." His narrow shoulders sagged and he turned back to his game.

"I'm sorry, sweetie. When I get home we'll go to the lake for a swim. I promise."

His face brightened a little. "Okay, Mom. See ya."

My heart ached. *What's happened to us?*

Bankruptcy had happened.

"I hate money," Adam said to me one night as I sat on the edge of his bed.

I almost wept. "I know, honey. I know this is hard."

I understood lost college and retirement funds weighed heavily on Paul, but we had lost more than that. What about joy? And fun? And happiness? I'd lost the man who always made me laugh when I was angry. The boys had lost the father who loved to act as much like a kid as they did.

As A.J. and I backed out of the driveway and headed down the dirt road I glanced at Paul, intent on the log before him.

I had to come up with a way to make a whole lot of money, so Paul would stop worrying and we'd be happy again.

Selling real estate wasn't going to do it. As a fledgling realtor in a small town swimming in realtors, I sold houses at the low end of the price spectrum. By the time the commission was divided, my piece was small. Besides, I hated selling real estate.

I need to start my own business.

I had no clue what starting and running a business would entail. I didn't even know enough to think that far ahead. I just knew I needed to make a lot of money and believed that owning a business was the way to do it. But we had settled into a life where naïve first steps into the unknown were — as far as my husband was concerned — reckless foolishness. Flying leaps? Not even up for discussion.

All that changed the day I decided to build a better brownie.

I grew up in a home where cooking was considered a tedious chore, and daily meals were basic and boring. Then I married a first-generation Italian, discovered the joys of sharing a wonderful meal, and realized I wanted to make great food. When a friend gave me a copy of *The Silver Palate Cookbook*, I jumped in. There were a few disasters, but I worked my way through a majority of the recipes, honing my skills and gradually gaining a reputation among family and friends as a good cook. Unfortunately, *The Silver Palate* was written before the words "heart-healthy" and "food" were used in the same sentence.

For years, I liberally laced dishes with butter and heavy cream without a second thought to arteries or waistlines. I started rethinking my heavy-handed ways when the world started counting fat grams instead of calories. "Low-fat" and "light" were the new buzzwords. The fat-free craze had begun.

Not wanting to be left at the station when the "Good Mother" train pulled out, I began studying nutritional labels and substituting yogurt and fat free sour cream for the fat-saturated ingredients I'd been using. I even tried changing the kid's favorite mac 'n' cheese and hot dogs to mac 'n' yogurt/cheese sauce and low-fat hot dogs. I found out you don't mess with classics.

Like the thick, chewy, fudgy brownies I made with a little help from my friend Betty Crocker. The secret was adding a handful — or two — of chocolate chips to Betty's mix along with the requisite oil and eggs. I was so addicted to these decadent morsels that, on more than one occasion, I lied and told my darling children the brownies were gone, when really I'd hidden the last few away for myself. But I was starting to pay for my dishonesty; my jeans were getting uncomfortably snug. When I had to resort to lying on the bed to get them zipped, I knew I was in trouble.

Skintight jeans on a mid-forties body made for painful walking as I shuffled to the pantry one afternoon and grabbed the resident box of mix. "Nine grams of fat in one piece? Who eats one?" And that was without the chocolate chips! I didn't have the willpower to cold-turkey off brownies, so I'd have to come up with a way to make them less deadly.

I changed into baggy sweatpants and headed back to the kitchen. "All right, girls." Two dogs raised their heads. "Time for healthy brownies!" I dumped the mix and a cup of plain, fat-free yogurt into a large bowl. The bag of chocolate chips stayed in the cupboard.

After pouring the batter into a pan and loading it into the oven, I cleaned up the kitchen. The baking brownies smelled as good as the bad-for-you ones. When the timer went off and I pulled the pan from the oven, they looked as good as the bad-for-you ones.

I cut a small corner piece, blew on it to cool it off, and then popped the warm morsel in my mouth. The chocolate flavor was predominant, but the sour tang of plain yogurt was loud and clear. *Damn.* I cut myself another piece — just to be sure.

Yogurt tang or not, the brownies disappeared. A couple of days later I tried again, this time with vanilla yogurt. Again they smelled and looked like the high-fat variety. But this time when I popped the corner piece in my mouth, sweet chocolate melted across my tongue. *Yum.*

I felt a nudge against my leg. Our flat-coated retriever, Maggie, was staring up at me, small droplets of drool shimmering around her mouth. "Kindred spirit, eh Mags?" I broke off a tiny corner for her and it disappeared. She looked back at me expectantly. "Sorry, girl. Chocolate's not good for dogs." Apparently not good for moms either, but that didn't seem to be stopping me. . . .

I grabbed the empty box from the counter. Total fat in just the mix was four grams for each brownie. Better than nine, but still not great. My eyes drifted to the ingredient list while my hand absently reached for the knife to cut another piece. *What's with the weird ingredients? "Dicalcium phosphate"? "Gellan gum"?*

Once I'd decided the path to family bliss was a business, "there must be something I can do" had become my mantra. It danced through my dreams, was my first thought in the morning, then shared my day like an imaginary friend. Hyperaware, I viewed the world as one big potential business opportunity waiting to happen. I was constantly scanning my day, expecting an epiphany to slap me upside the head and scream: *That's it!*

But standing in my kitchen, steadily feeding myself one little piece of warm brownie after another, there was no epiphany, no clanging bells. I just felt a quiet glimmer. *I bet I'm not the only one who wants brownies without all the fat and ingredients I can't pronounce.*

A few days later, I was flipping through a magazine when a product review on a fat-free, ready-made brownie caught my eye. Someone had stolen my idea!

I picked the boys up after school and headed to the store. "New Item!" proclaimed the shelf tag. I ripped the box open as I walked back to the car and handed each boy a piece.

"Yuck." A.J. dropped what was left of his brownie into my outstretched hand.

"Tastes like raisins." Adam's face screwed up in distaste. I read the side panel; one of the main ingredients was "prune puree." Who says my kids don't have discerning palates?

I stuffed the partially eaten brownies back in the package and stared down at the ripped carton. The kids' voices seemed to fade. The car wheels weren't turning, but the ones in my brain were.

I can do better. I'll make low-fat brownies with yogurt and only normal brownie ingredients. I'll . . ."

"Mom?"

Huh?

"MOM!"

I came back to the parking lot with a jolt.

"What're we doing?"

"You mean you don't want to sit here all afternoon? How 'bout ice cream?"

"Yippee!"

Their voices faded again as I headed for the ice cream store.

I'll make enough money to pay for the kid's college educations. That should make Paul feel better. They're only in third and fifth grades; I have plenty of time.

For the rest of the week I fantasized about the successful company I was going to start and the big bucks I was going to make. I didn't give one moment's consideration to how I was going to do this, I just was.

Talk about audacity . . .

I had no life experience for what was coming. My father was an artist without a business bone in his body and my mother had worked one unskilled job after another to keep the family afloat. I had gone to a three-year nursing school, worked in a big-city emergency room, and then was a happy, stay-at-home mom for nine years. Not exactly the road map for a successful entrepreneur.

When Paul got home on Friday night I managed to contain myself while he greeted the boys and changed into jeans. He poured himself a scotch and leaned against the kitchen counter. "How was your day?"

"Well. . . I've got this great idea for a business!" I launched into the story of the mix and the yogurt and the yucky prune brownies. The grand finale was my announcement that I was going to start a business to sell low-fat brownies to the masses.

"Whoa!" He straightened up. "A business? What about real estate?"

Real estate? "Oh, I'll keep selling real estate too. I'll do this on the side."

"We need your real-estate income."

"I know." *I hate real estate.*

Reassured, he leaned against the counter again and took a swallow of his scotch. "I guess it's an interesting idea, but why would anyone buy a low-fat brownie? I mean, if you don't want the fat, don't eat 'em."

I rolled my eyes. "You are such a guy."

"Can't argue with that." He reached for the bowl of nuts that had miraculously appeared next to his scotch. "But really, how do you know there's a market for something like this?" He tossed a handful of peanuts into his mouth.

"I can't be the only one who wants a product like this, or someone else wouldn't already be doing it." I grinned. "Luckily, theirs are gross."

"I guess it's worth looking into." Straightening up, he grabbed the bowl and his scotch and turned towards the living room. "I'm gonna watch the news. What's for supper?"

Not exactly a ringing endorsement, but I interpreted it as a supportive "Go for it!"

My body went back to making dinner, but my mind went back to my fantasies. I was gonna make low-fat, fudgy brownies the world would love.

Only one small detail stood in the way of certain success. A recipe. Or lack thereof. . .

The following week I researched brownie recipes, bought ingredients, and started telling friends and family about my new business idea. The responses varied from skeptical — "Low-fat brownies?" — to vacant smiles accompanied by "Interesting. . . ." My excitement began to diminish. I procrastinated, vacillated, and accomplished little.

Then, in one defining, vividly remembered moment, everything changed.

The boys and I were having our drive-to-school conversation one October morning when Adam announced, "There are tryouts for a radio show after school, but I don't think I'm gonna go."

I looked at him in the rearview mirror. "Why not?"

"Because I know I won't make it." He wasn't upset or disappointed, just matter-of-fact.

My response was instant and intuitive, "Sweetie, there is nothing wrong with failing. What's wrong is when you don't even try."

I almost drove off the road.

I don't know if some higher power was trying to get my attention, or if my subconscious was playing back what I wanted to hear, but it hit me like a thunderbolt.

I'm supposed to be showing them how to be brave and risk failure, rather than telling them how.

I dropped the kids off at school, went home and started baking brownies.

Chapter 2

I spent hours in my kitchen, making pans of brownies at breakneck speed. I'd never created a recipe from scratch. I took copious notes on each batch as it was carefully evaluated by my official taste-testers.

You know, the two guys who arrived every morning in their pickup trucks, wearing John Deere hats and carrying coffee from the local mini-mart. The same ones who were sawing boards and hammering nails outside my kitchen. We'd decided to turn an enclosed porch area into a back hall and hired two local contractors for the job. The self-proclaimed chocoholics were only too happy to take several brownie-breaks a day.

"Ready!" Immediately the pounding stopped and they came trooping into a kitchen filled with the seductive smell of baking brownies. Hands washed, coffee refilled, we gathered around the pans on the kitchen island. I placed a piece from each of the two slightly different batches on napkins marked "1" and "2."

They each took a piece from napkin "1" and it disappeared in one bite. Their eyes narrowed as they chewed slowly, focusing on the flavors in their mouths.

"Okay, got it," Mark nodded. Both "cleansed their palates" with a deep slug of coffee, then reached for "2," repeating the process.

"So?" I asked.

"Number '2' is too sweet. Not enough chocolate comes through," Mark stated. Jim solemnly agreed.

"Number '1' has good chocolate flavor, but is still too cakey." They both nodded.

I carefully adjusted the sugar, cocoa, or baking soda and tried again. I made and threw away more pans of brownies than any ten people make in a lifetime, but by the time Mark and Jim packed up their tools, I had a great new back hall and a recipe for brownies that were low in fat and made without additives or preservatives. And, more importantly, brownies my fussy taste-testers didn't think were too sweet, too cakey, or not chocolaty enough. They were just right — fudgy and delicious.

I was elated, excited, and ready to take the next step. Only I had no idea what the next step should be. . . .

I knew Paul could point me in the right direction, but reaching out to him would open an already cracked hornets' nest. Initially he'd humored me, but then watched my baking marathon with growing concern. He was away for most of it, but on those days when he worked from home, it was impossible to ignore.

Walking into the kitchen, empty coffee cup in hand, he surveyed the chaos. With a tight smile, he made his way to the coffee pot through the maze of mixing bowls, bags and boxes of ingredients, measuring cups and pans.

"A batch is about to come out of the oven. Want to try 'em?"

He shook his head. "I've got a conference call." A pause, and then the inevitable "You going into the office today?"

Damn it. A cold twist of resentment hit the pit of my stomach. "I'm going in after lunch."

"Good." He headed back down the hall to his office. "See ya later."

Where I saw money-making, he saw money-devouring. The more enthusiastic I got, the more he withdrew. When avoidance was impossible, the conversation always ended up about my real-estate income. I felt guilty, then resentful, and I withdrew. The air between us was thick with tension.

One night after the kids had inhaled their dinners and gone to watch TV, we sat at the table, finishing a glass of wine. These few minutes had always been a relaxing time to chat about our lives; this was where the connection was renewed. But lately the connection had been awkward, strained. And the longer we danced around the 800-pound gorilla standing in the middle of the room, the more frustrated I became.

With a "what the Hell, might as well get this over with" attitude, I ventured forward. "I need to figure out the next step for my business."

He put down his wine glass and looked at me. "You're finally starting to make enough money to help pay the bills." His voice was tight with suppressed anger. "Why start a business doing something you know absolutely nothing about?"

"I can learn," I said with naively foolish, yet stubborn, certainty. "I can do this."

"You don't know that." His dark brown eyes were intense. "It costs a lot of money to start a business. Money we don't have. Besides, I'm gone all week and don't have time to help you."

I couldn't deny he was making good if not excellent points, none of which I had a rational argument for.

He took the last swallow of his wine and angrily pushed back his chair, "This is an added stress I don't need."

Rational flew out the window. The hornets' nest ripped wide open and began swinging wildly.

"What about me? It's my turn, I've always supported you." My fists were clenched. "Why can't you support me?"

"Want to know why I can't support you?" he snapped. "Because you're being unreasonable and irresponsible."

What had begun as a quest to make him happier had become something very different. This was no longer about Paul. It was about me. Raised in a family that believed a college education was a waste of time and money for girls, my sister and I were supposed to learn a "trade" to fill time while we lived at home and waited for a man on a white horse to come along. He would pull us up behind him and carry us away to be sheltered and cared for because, as women, we were incapable of taking care of ourselves.

Paul had been raised the same way.

By the time we started dating, neither of us had lived at home since high school. I was twenty-nine and considered myself an independent woman; he was thirty and considered himself a liberated man. But certain beliefs were ingrained. After we married and the boys were born, we slipped unconsciously into the roles our families had prepared us for.

Now, eleven years later, I was rebelling. The timing may have sucked, but I couldn't turn my feelings off any more than I could stop the wind. I was forty-four years old and finally believed I could do and be more than I had been raised to believe. I was finding my voice and wanted — no, *needed* — to be heard.

At the time, I was not self-aware enough to understand what was going on with either of us. My brilliant insight into the whys and wherefores is pure hindsight. All I knew was that I was pissed. And so was he. So much for making the family happy again. . .

We did the dishes in angry silence.

It felt like we were entering a dark tunnel and neither one of us knew how to find our way out.

Chapter 3

After our angry dinner conversation, the topic of my upstart business became, by unspoken agreement, off-limits. Unless one of us had a dramatic change of heart, we'd reached an impasse. As the days slid by, my frustration grew and with it my anger and resentment.

Then I came up with an idea.

I read an article in *Inc.* magazine that showcased a California couple with a small tofu company. They had received a year of free business guidance from a volunteer organization called SCORE (Service Corp of Retired Executives). A couple of SCORE counselors had helped them acquire the business "savvy" they were lacking. Since "savvy" was one of the many things I was lacking, SCORE seemed like the place for me.

"I'll make a deal with you," I offered on my nightly phone call with Paul. "I'll go to SCORE and get an objective, unbiased opinion. If the person there thinks I'm getting in over my head or my idea won't fly, I'll drop it. But, if they think my idea is a good one, I'll go ahead." I felt comfortable offering this deal because I believed with all my heart that my idea was so good, anyone — other than him — would see the potential and enthusiastically encourage me to move forward.

Paul agreed because he believed just as strongly that any person with business expertise would listen to my plan and tell me that it wasn't viable or that my lack of experience made it too risky.

For the moment there was an uneasy truce.

The man who answered the phone at SCORE suggested I sign up for their next "How to Start a Business" seminar, in a couple of weeks.

But I'm ready now! "I'd like to see someone sooner than that." *Got anything later today?*

He had an opening later in the week. "Bring your business plan and financials so your counselor can review them."

Huh? "I'm afraid I don't have a business plan or financials." I tried hard to sound self-assured, the exact opposite of what I felt. "I'm in the very early stages of this business and those are things I need help with." There was a pause during which I realized I was holding my breath.

"No business plan or financials?" I imagined him thinking. "What kind of idiot do I have on the phone?" Instead the voice, kinder now, said, "No problem, just bring whatever you have."

I hung up the phone, not sure if I was excited or terrified. I was beginning to realize how little I knew about what I so blithely believed I could do. I breezily told Paul about the appointment, never mentioning the details of the conversation or my doubts. Admit uncertainty and face the inevitable "I told you so"? Never.

I took brownies. Maybe I didn't have a business plan or financials, but I had great brownies. I figured I'd knock the counselor's socks off with those and he would be so excited that he would immediately want to teach me all the business stuff I didn't know.

On the day of the appointment, the hilly terrain on either side of the highway looked bleak under a steel-gray November sky. I pulled into downtown Lebanon, New Hampshire, parked the car, and took a deep breath before gathering the brownies and stepping out into the cold, damp air. I pulled my coat tighter and headed across the large town square.

The SCORE office was on the second floor of a bank building facing the square. My butterflies and I rode the elevator to the second floor, got off, and found the correct door.

An older gentleman looked up from a desk in the small reception area.

"May I help you?" he asked.

"My name is Lindsay Frucci. I have an appointment at 11:00."

"Welcome." His smile was warm. "Your appointment's with Dave Johnson." He pushed back his chair and stood. "Let me show you where you'll be meeting."

He escorted me into the conference room. Then he excused himself.

I placed the brownies on the table and sat to wait. The butterflies were multiplying.

"Lindsay?" A slender, dark-haired man was walking towards me. "I'm Dave Johnson." He extended his hand. "Sorry to have kept you waiting."

We settled across the table from each other.

"Tell me about your business idea."

As I explained, I offered him a brownie. He took a bite and offered a noncommittal "Very good." Though he maintained eye contact, his face was expressionless, impossible to read.

When I was done, he asked business-type questions about money and manufacturing and market research — questions I didn't have answers for. The butterflies turned to knots.

He switched gears.

"Is being home with your young sons important to you?" *Well, duh — of course it is.*

"Is your husband around to help with the kids?" *Not exactly. . .*

The final blow came, carefully aimed and fired, "What does your husband think of your idea? Is he supportive?" The trap was sprung and I was caught.

Ohmygod. This guy is Paul's clone.

He leaned back in his chair and folded his hands. "I'm really sorry," he shook his head, "but I have to be honest. I think this is too much for you. My suggestion is you stick to being a mother and maybe think about this again when your boys are older." He could not have been more patronizing if he had patted me on the head.

This can't be happening.

Clone Guy looked uncomfortable as I stood and began gathering my things. I had to get out of there before I started to cry. Or scratched his condescending little eyes out.

"Hold on a second." He pushed back his chair. "Someone just walked in who might want to hear your idea." He was probably worried about being alone with a weepy, pissed-off woman. Smart man. "He worked in the food industry. Let me see if he's got a minute." He hurried from the room.

I sat down, happy for a reprieve — no matter how uncertain its outcome might be.

When Bob Fox walked through the door, he didn't look like what I imagined an angel would look like. He was in his early sixties, medium height and balding, with kind, intelligent eyes behind rimless glasses. He offered a warm smile and a firm handshake, then sat down across the table and immediately reached for a brownie.

"May I?" He took a big bite and started to chew. His eyes widened and a surprised look spread across his face. "These are really good! They're low-fat?"

Now this was the reaction I'd been looking for!

"I think so. They're made with yogurt and they're all natural."

He reached for another one and leaned back in his chair. "Tell me your business idea."

This time the person I talked to was engaged and interested. He nodded. "It's a great idea."

I honestly don't remember saying a word; I just sat there and grinned. Then he asked if I knew what the next steps should be.

Uh oh, here we go. I admitted that I didn't.

Instead of looking shocked, he simply nodded. "We have another member, Jay Albert, who just retired as president of a specialty food company," he said. "Can I give him your number?"

"Are you kidding? That would be great!"

I gave Bob the rest of the brownies to take home.

To say Bob had "worked in the food industry" was an understatement. He'd been a senior executive with General Foods for twenty years. I floated to my car.

About half way home the steel sky began spitting snowflakes. As if in reaction, my euphoria began to dissipate and I felt the first icy quiver of doubt.

Since my driving-the-kids-to-school epiphany, I had felt empowered and confident. Through the dark cloud of Paul's obvious disapproval and my frustration at my friends' skeptical responses, I held on to my belief that I could make this business happen. I had become increasingly determined to prove everyone wrong. My confidence should have been boosted by the fact that I now had an objective, unbiased supporter in Bob — but that's exactly what scared me to death.

Okay, girl, you've been "talking the talk." Now someone who knows what he's doing thinks you can "walk the walk."

Although I couldn't see Paul's face during our call that night, it didn't take a psychic to know he was unhappy.

"I'd like to know what all this is gonna cost." Abrupt and annoyed.

"That's something we have to work on. Please don't be so negative."

"We don't have money to throw away."

Really? Didn't know that. . .

After the kids went to bed, I crawled under the covers with a book. I didn't want to think about brownies anymore. I just wanted to read a chapter and go to sleep. But when I realized I'd read the same paragraph three times, I gave up and turned out the light. Other than an occasional dog snore, the only sound in the dark room was the voice in my head.

I've been so sure this was right for us. What if I'm wrong? Fear urged the doubt along. *I don't know anything about starting a business. Bob is clearly a nice man; what right do I have to waste his time?*

It was a long night. I began to believe what others did — that I wasn't capable or smart enough. I wasn't strong or determined enough.

What am I trying to prove? I'm a good mother — that should be enough.

The road that had seemed so straight and clear slipped from view.

I didn't voice my doubts to anyone. Verbalizing them would have been painful and made them real. I'm sure Paul was relieved when I let the subject drop. If I was finally coming to my senses, that was fine with him.

A few days after my SCORE meeting, Jay called and suggested we meet. I politely told him that with the upcoming holidays, my schedule was too busy and I would call him in a couple of weeks.

I never did.

This story could easily have ended right here. I believed the naysayers knew me better than I knew myself. I entered 1995 with a determination to forget brownies and focus on real estate.

Then one morning in mid-January, Jay called again.

"I haven't heard from you and wondered if you wanted to try and schedule that meeting?"

I held on to my resolve. "I've been giving this some thought and don't think I'm going to move forward." The self-sabotage was complete.

But Jay wasn't buying it. "Listen, Bob thinks you have a great idea. Why not just get together and have a conversation?" He wasn't leaving me any wiggle room. "There's no obligation. If, after we meet, you still don't want to move forward, that's fine." There was a slight pause. "What do you say?"

The universe was delivering a strong message. If I chose to ignore this "slap upside the head," that was my prerogative, but I couldn't say I hadn't been warned.

I agreed to meet. We set a date for the following week.

Jay has no memory of this conversation. It may have been insignificant to him, but it would change my life.

Chapter 4

I arrived at the SCORE office armed with a pan of brownies and a serious case of nerves. Bob greeted me warmly and then introduced me to Jay, another sixty-something gentleman with a slight stoop and a warm smile. We'd barely settled in our chairs when Jay looked at me intently and fired the first question.

"Let's say you decide to go ahead and sell your brownies. Do you want a business or a hobby?"

My reply was automatic. "A business." I may not have known what running a business involved, but I knew I wanted one. Or had wanted one. Or something. . .

"So what you're saying is," he said, his gaze never wavering, "you want to produce a product to sell in grocery stores across the country, as opposed to baking brownies in your kitchen and selling them locally."

I nodded. *Yup, that's what I want. Sell my brownies all over the country, make lots of money, send my kids to college, prove my husband wrong, learn something, have fun, and whatever else you say.*

With an "alright then, let's roll up our sleeves and get to work" nod, Jay looked from me to Bob and back. "Then the first thing we need to do is run the numbers."

We? Did he say "we"?

With their matter-of-fact acceptance, these two men erased all my doubts. If I was serious, they were serious. I was back in full-speed-ahead mode.

"Step one," Jay continued, "is cost of goods. Have you thought about using a co-packer?"

Given that I had no idea what a co-packer was, I hadn't thought about using one.

"A co-packer's a company that uses their equipment to manufacture products for other companies," Bob explained. "The key is to find someone who makes products using the same equipment you'll need for your brownies."

"I assumed I'd make them myself." I looked at both men. "I've looked into the cost of buying a used mixer."

Jay raised his eyebrows. "Do you have room in your home for a manufacturing area?"

In my 200-year-old farmhouse? "Uh, not really."

He pushed his glasses up on his nose. "Do you have the money to build a manufacturing facility?"

"No."

"Do you know anything about manufacturing?"

The volleys were coming hard and fast. I was starting to squirm. "No."

"What do you see as your role?" He was relentless. "Do you want to work the manufacturing line or grow the business?"

"Grow the business?"

He threw his hands in the air. "Then why on earth would you want to manufacture this yourself?"

Point and match. "Guess I don't."

My new best friends spent the next two hours giving me my first "Business 101" class. They talked; I listened, asked questions, and took notes furiously. I had lots to learn.

I left with a long to-do list and a plan to meet again in two weeks. My head was spinning, but I was excited. I'd finally found the support I'd been longing for.

Standing in the kitchen before dinner that night, I cautiously told Paul that the brownie business had been revived. I wasn't expecting cartwheels, but neither was I ready for the intensity of his sharp, angry look. Any warmth I'd carried home from my meeting evaporated in the chilly silence.

Ladies and gentlemen, the 800-pound gorilla is back in the house.

"What do you think about switching to a dry mix?" Jay asked at our next meeting.

My plan was to sell oven-ready, frozen batter. "If I did a mix, the consumer would have to add yogurt, eggs, and vanilla."

"You can get dry egg whites," Bob said. "And there are ways to add small amounts of liquid such as vanilla to a dry mix."

"I'll bet you could get dried yogurt solids as well." Jay said. "Then they'd only have to add water."

"I'm not crazy about the idea of adding water." I paused a second to let the thoughts flying through my brain form into words. "What about a mix with egg whites and vanilla in it, but the consumer adds the yogurt? They'd feel like they were adding something healthy and it would be unique."

"Great idea!" Bob slapped the table enthusiastically.

Jay was nodding. "I like it."

I was released with my trusty to-do list — which included finding the dry ingredients I needed and redoing my recipe.

The icy February wind stung as I left the warm building. I pulled the collar of my jacket tightly around my chin and headed towards the car. When the just-add-yogurt idea popped into my brain and out of my mouth, Jay and Bob had simply accepted it as a great idea, but I'd been stunned. What surprised me even more was how sure of it I was.

I arrived home full of energy. I couldn't wait to start on my list, but two boys were getting out of school, and by the time they were in bed, I'd be pooped. The "me" part of my day was over and family time was about to jump into full swing.

It had been a big day and I wanted to share it with Paul. I convinced myself that maybe, just maybe, this would be the turning point. The just-add-yogurt idea was *so* cool that when he heard it, he'd have to be impressed.

The boys and I were sitting at the table chatting over the last bites of dinner when he called. I answered the phone and told him about the meeting.

"I came up with the idea to make it a 'just-add-yogurt' dry mix!"

"That's nice, but listen, I've got to get back into this meeting. I'd better say goodnight to the boys."

A cold rock settled in my stomach.

"Okay, here's Adam. I'll see you tomorrow night."

After the boys were in bed, I sat and stared into the fire. When I realized tears were running down my cheeks I angrily brushed them away. I wasn't sure which emotion was winning the battle raging within. Anger? Or fear?

I went to bed feeling very alone.

Chapter 5

"Hey Mom!" I woke with a start. Adam's grinning face was at the passenger window. He climbed into the front seat. "You were snoring."

"Was not."

"And your mouth was open, just like Auntie Leslie." My sister is known for her "fly-catching" naps.

"Cute." I rolled my eyes at him. "This stays between us, kiddo."

"Sure. You, me, Kevin, and Mrs. D." He nodded past me. I turned to see Kevin and my friend Sue, a.k.a. Kevin's Mom, standing there laughing. *Busted.* I rolled down the window.

"Tired much?" Sue asked.

"Ya think?"

"Mom, can Kevin come over?"

I raised my eyebrows at Sue.

"It's fine with me," she nodded, "except I have to go to Concord, so I can't pick him up."

"I'll drive him home." The Davises lived five minutes from us.

Before Sue could respond A.J. came running to the car. "Can Chris come over he already asked his mother and she said yes hi Mrs. D." All in one breathe.

I looked across the parking lot to where Chris's mom was standing. I gave her a thumbs-up.

"I told her you'd drive him home," A.J. announced. I closed my eyes. *You have* got *to be kidding.* Chris lived twenty minutes from our house.

I turned to see Sue looking at me.

"How about coffee in the morning?" She suggested. "I want to hear how the new mix is coming along."

"It'd be coming along great if I had some time to work on it." I ran my fingers through my hair. "Coffee sounds great."

The next morning, I carried my latte to one of the tables lined up along the large windows in our favorite meeting place. The smell of baking bagels and brewing coffee, mingling with small-town chatter, made for a cozy gathering place on a cold winter morning.

I plopped into the chair across from Sue. "I needed this."

"You look exhausted."

"Gee, thanks."

She tipped her head and eyeballed me. "So what's goin' on?"

"I'm going in fifteen different directions, that's all." I took a sip of my latte and closed my eyes. When I opened them, a bagel with a healthy schmear of cream cheese had materialized on the table. “Thanks, Case.”

Casey, the owner, looked at me with concern. “You okay? You look tired.”

I slumped down in my chair and laughed. “Maybe I should go back to bed and start all over again.”

She patted me on the shoulder and headed back behind the counter.

“So really, how’s the new formula?” Sue was one of the few people who had supported my idea from the beginning. Because she owned and ran her own business, she was a valuable sounding board.

“I’m spending mornings at the real-estate office, but I’ve been sneaking out early, which isn’t going unnoticed. Even then, I only have time to get one batch done before I have to pick up the kids.” I took a bite of my bagel. “This sucks.” I managed around a mouthful.

Sue raised her eyebrows.

“Not the bagel. Life.”

She nodded. “What’s Paul’s attitude these days?”

I took a long swallow of latte. “Not good.” I put the cup down. “Here’s the thing . . . his biggest problem is money. So I figure I’ll pay for everything with my real-estate commissions.”

“Good idea.”

“But I’ve gotta have real-estate commissions in order to do that, and the only way to make them is to put in more hours. The more hours I put in at the office, the fewer I have to work on the brownies. Oh, and did I mention kids, dogs, housework, grocery shopping, and laundry?” I leaned back in my chair. “I’m screwed.”

She laughed. "You'll pull it off."

Since I didn't have the luxury of my carpenter/taste-testers anymore, I figured my two darling sons would be happy to step in. But no, not my ungrateful little thugs. Clearly, the idea of being "brownie guinea pigs" didn't appeal to them. They'd walk in the door after school, starving as always, and ask for a snack.

"How about a brownie?" I'd sweetly suggest.

What started as a firm "no thank you" soon became a drawn out "Mommmm!" punctuated with groans and rolling of eyes. I stopped offering before their refusals reached the point of running from the room screaming.

Yet even with a tight time schedule and uncooperative taste-testers, it wasn't long before I created a "just-add-yogurt" dry mix. I finally had a real product around which to start building a real business.

"Lindsay, these are great!" Bob was positively glowing.

Jay's "Congratulations, you did it!" was delivered with a big smile.

I was back at SCORE sitting across from my personal cheering squad.

"Now," Jay said, "we need to get a nutritional analysis done."

God I love coming here. Sitting with these two men, I felt important, respected, valued. But the wonderful support I received here magnified the lack of support at home. Support I ached for. While their official mission was to help me feed fudgy, "better for you" brownies to the masses, their unwitting mission was to feed my heart and soul.

"How do we do that?" Using my calculator and the nutritional information on each ingredient, I had come up with what I thought was the caloric and fat content. Unfortunately the FDA required an analysis that was a tad more scientific.

"There's a lab in Boston that's fast, reliable, and not too expensive." Jay passed over the contact information. "Call and see what they need in order to do an analysis. They'll tell you the FDA requirements for 'low-fat.'"

Bob spoke up. "You need to do a trademark search as soon as you come up with a name. And you need to think about incorporating."

Jay was back. "Start keeping track of cash flow and we can work on projections of what all this is going to cost."

Cash flow. Projections. That meant numbers. . . . Whenever anyone tried to "speak math" with me I immediately felt an unreasonable but nonetheless real-to-me panic. I was one of those girls who'd accepted early on that I was incapable of understanding numbers. But Bob and Jay refused to believe I was incapable of learning anything (dear, wonderful men). They began the tortuous task of teaching me how to understand the financial aspects of my business.

There aren't words to convey how agonizing these sessions were for me and how patient Jay and Bob were. Years later when Stuart became my third SCORE counselor and the painful numbers conversations were still going on, he too, was always ready to explain something *one more time.* I learned it all. It wasn't easy and I was never fluent, but I learned how to "read" numbers and to speak the language enough to understand what they said about the health of my business.

I left that day with my usual to-do list. If the fat level didn't fall within the FDA's definition of low-fat, the viability of my business would be questionable. When I got home, I contacted the lab, shipped them both baked brownies and mix as instructed, then sat back and waited.

Chapter 6

The call came the following Friday. I'd left the real-estate office at noon and headed home. Once in the door, I gave belly rubs and behind-the-ear scratches to two attention-starved pups and checked my messages.

"Lindsay, this is Amy from Food Labs. I have your results. Give me a call."

My heart raced. I took a deep breath and punched the numbers.

"You sitting down?" Amy asked.

Oh God. . . "Should I be?"

"Don't worry, it's good news." She paused. "Your brownies aren't low-fat."

"You said good news."

"They're fat-free."

"Excuse me?"

"They're under the FDA requirement of less than .5 grams of fat per serving. And they're only 120 calories each. Considering a regular brownie usually starts at 7 grams of fat and 150 calories, it's great news."

"I can't believe this. Thank you so much."

"Hey, all I did was the analysis. You made the brownies. Good luck with your business!"

Fat-free? This was beyond my wildest dreams. After she hung up, I dialed the phone again.

"Guess what? The brownies are fat-free!"

"You're kidding!" Paul sounded as surprised as I'd been. "That's awesome, honey — congratulations." There was actually a tinge of interest in his voice.

One short call from Amy had made it a wonderful day. One short conversation with Paul had made it perfect. I told myself we'd turned the corner. With this news, he had to see the potential.

The next day Paul and I found ourselves in the car alone. Being alone on a Saturday afternoon was unusual enough, but the mood was lighter than it had been in a long time.

"So. . ." I ventured. "I need a name for my company."

"Hmm. . ." He frowned thoughtfully. "Lindsay's Luscious Brownies?"

"I don't think so."

"I know! Frucci's Fantastic Brownies." He glanced at me, a smile lit up his face and the little lines around his eyes crinkled.

"Ah. . ." I was smiling so hard, my cheeks hurt. "No."

"Well, they're fat-free, how about 'No Pudge'? You know — *pudge* as in *fat*? "

"That's kinda cute."

"You could put the line across the O in "no" like they have on the signs." He was on a roll. "Your logo could be a skinny pig with a tape measure around its waist."

I tried it on for size. "No Pudge." I started to laugh. "I like it."

"Yeah?"

"So if the brownies are "No Pudge", what would you call the company?"

"I'd keep it simple." He tilted his head, considering. "How about No Pudge Foods?"

"No Pudge Brownies and No Pudge Foods." I envisioned a cute, skinny pig with a tape measure around its waist. It felt humorously, don't-take-yourself-too-seriously right.

He looked at me with a big grin. "Am I good or what?"

"You're good, honey. I gotta admit, you are good."

Bob and Jay loved the new name and logo idea. Bob immediately started clicking out a new to-do list. "Get your logo idea down so we can do a trademark search and get that and the name registered. You need to incorporate. How's the co-packer search coming?"

"Huh?" I'd been taking notes furiously. "Um, slowly." In other words, it's not. . . .

"Lindsay." Bob's tone was unusually serious. "Finding the right co-packer should be your top priority. Without that, you have no business."

"Top priority" usually translated into "time-consuming," which, with my schedule, translated into "stressful," which then led to nights of staring at the ceiling, trying to figure out the fastest way to get the damn thing done, so that I could get it off the damn list. But as soon as I did, I would find another "top priority" task waiting to take its place.

As a friend of mine who owned his own business said when he heard I was about to take the leap, "So now you'll be working part-time." I was about to agree when he asked, "Which twelve-hour shift you working?"

I laughed. He didn't.

Chapter 7

I have come to believe the universe has, and is willing to share, the answers to most of our questions. I'm not sure I'm talking about God. Maybe I am. Whatever you want to call it, I believe a force exists that will gently guide us through life if we allow ourselves to be open to the messages. It can be as simple as feeling happy. Or that nagging feeling that something's "not right." Other times the message manifests as a life experience.

Looking back I realize I'd been receiving messages for a while. One example was my first meeting at SCORE. After being discouraged and dismissed by the first counselor, Clone Guy heard a voice in the outer office and invited Bob into my life. What if Bob had arrived five minutes later? Then there was the follow-up phone call from Jay — an out-of-the blue, unsolicited call encouraging me to "just get together and talk" at a time when my resolve and self-confidence had slipped away.

Those events, combined with what unfolded next, make me believe that a force or the universe or God or something was reassuring me and, in essence, saying loud and clear, "You're headed in the right direction, keep moving forward."

I was in the produce aisle of the grocery store, when I bumped into a former classmate from nursing school. Standing by the tomatoes and cucumbers, I gave her a rundown of No Pudge, finishing with my need for a graphic artist to do logo and package design.

"My husband's a graphic artist." She stopped picking through the green beans. "You should give him a call."

"You don't remember me, do you?" Lee said when I called him the next afternoon. "You're John Head's daughter, right?"

My father was a fine-arts painter and much older than Lee. It turned out Lee had attended the art school in Boston where my father had taught. When he first arrived, fresh from rural Vermont, my father had recognized a lonely country boy and taken him under his wing.

"I even went to your house for dinner a couple of times. I think you were in junior high."

I didn't remember meeting him, but it didn't matter, the connection was there. We set a date to meet at his studio.

If the way to a man's heart was through his stomach, I reasoned the way to a man's artistic soul had to be through chocolate. At our first meeting I fed Lee freshly baked, No Pudge brownies and got exactly the results I'd hoped for. Not only was he excited about the brownies, he "got" my vision so clearly that within a week, color mock-ups of three smiling, skinny piggies were spread across the table in his bright, under-the-eaves studio.

"I like this one," I pointed to the one standing in profile with its head turned looking at me and grinning from ear to ear. A yellow tape measure was wrapped around its waist. "I love how colorful and fun this is! I can't wait to see it on a label."

A week later I was looking at the mock-up of a predominately pink label with my smiling, skinny pig standing proudly atop big letters that said "NO PUDGE."

"It's awesome."

Lee raised his eyebrows. "It's definitely different."

"Which is exactly what I wanted. It'll attract attention!" I studied it again. "I think we should put an exclamation point at the end of 'No Pudge.' Whaddya think?"

I didn't understand it at the time, but the decisions I made about the logo and packaging were my first big marketing decisions and they were spot-on. It would be a long time before I acknowledged that I had an instinct for marketing, but once I began to trust it, that instinct served me well.

Sitting in Lee's neat-as-a-pin studio late one afternoon, I watched as he intently moved images and type between two computer screens with the flick of his mouse.

"Do you want your title to be President on your business card?" he asked.

"You're kidding, right? That sounds so weird."

"What did you put down for your title when you incorporated?"

"'President, Vice President, and Secretary' — but you're not putting that on a business card. President just sounds so . . . presumptuous."

"I'll do whatever you want, but I think it should be President."

No Pudge! Foods, Inc.
Lindsay H. Frucci, President

Cool.

Soon after our company-naming moment of harmony, Paul's tight-lipped disapproval resurfaced. I couldn't identify why the upward swing had crashed, but the 800-pound gorilla was back. I prayed it would stay home when we left to meet friends in Munich on our first vacation in years.

The excitement of taking the train from Zurich to Munich, combined with the anticipation of spending time with a great group of people, got the trip off to a fantastic start. As we rolled past quaint villages and flower-filled meadows, it seemed my prayer had been answered.

Monika, my friend in Munich, couldn't wait to hear all the details about No Pudge! and brought it up our first night. Immediately, the gorilla charged into the room. I changed the subject as quickly as possible, but it was too late. Paul was clearly annoyed.

For the next five days we were rarely alone. We pushed the ape to the background and tried to pretend he hadn't made an appearance. After a great visit, we left Munich and our friends and took the train back to Zurich for the last day of our trip.

We spent the morning window-shopping along modern Zurich's wide boulevards lined with elegant boutiques and art galleries, and then we crossed into the old city. As night fell, we had a wonderful dinner at a sidewalk café on a narrow cobblestone street. Holding hands, we strolled through the warm spring night, determined to ignore the dark presence lumbering along at our heels, growing impatient with being ignored. When we settled on a bench next to Lake Zurich, the good feelings of the past week, combined with a couple glasses of wine and the beautiful surroundings, lulled me into thinking it was time to invite the gorilla to join us. I hoped that by acknowledging his presence we could banish him.

"Goddamn it! Can we not talk about your stupid company?"

That moment will stay with me forever. The hurtful words had been said before, but the raw intensity was new.

"I don't know why you can't support me." Tears streamed down my cheeks.

"Because you're being incredibly selfish." A deep scowl darkened Paul's face. "I don't want you to do this."

"You're the one being selfish. No Pudge! has the potential to be a successful company."

"Does it? You have no idea what you're doing. We're just getting ourselves to the point where we might be able to feel secure and now you want to start a company and put that stability at risk? And I'm being selfish?" He was furious.

Angry words, tears, and more angry words, until we were drained and empty. We walked back to the hotel in silence, the dark presence between us. It joined us in the cab to the airport the next morning and settled in for the long, silent flight home.

Chapter 8

Once we were home, I focused on nailing down a co-packer. Until that was accomplished, No Pudge! was going nowhere. After Zurich, "going nowhere" wasn't an option.

A co-packer that had sounded promising on the phone turned out to be one room of partially automated equipment. Ingredients and packaging were stacked along the walls in a haphazard fashion and a coating of flour dust covered everything, including the floor. It was a short visit.

The highway home sliced through rolling Vermont hills. Spring was emerging and covering the bucolic scenery with its pale green beauty. I barely noticed.

I need a fully automated plant. With high quality control standards! A place big enough to handle growth. I'd outgrow the place I just saw in a year!

Talk about chutzpah! I never considered that a co-packer of the size I wanted might not want me: a one-woman start-up with a recipe and — oh yeah — no customers.

Thanks to play dates and business travel, a couple of days later I was blessed with a long afternoon to myself. Determined not to let this rare block of time go to waste, I sat at the kitchen table with the name and number of a new co-packer.

I placed the call and explained why I was calling three times before finally being transferred to the president of the company.

"Do you know what time it is?" he asked.

"Uh. . ."

"It's almost five o'clock on Friday afternoon. Not the best time to call if you want someone to take time with you." His words could easily have been a reprimand but sounded more like friendly advice.

"I'm sorry. I lost track of time."

"Well, you're in luck — I have a few minutes to spare."

We talked for almost an hour. Finally he said, "I know exactly who should pack this for you." The large manufacturing facility he had in mind maintained strict quality controls and could handle whatever growth No Pudge! threw at it.

"Tell Peter I said he needs to do this for you. If he doesn't say 'yes,' call me back and I'll talk to him."

"I don't know how to thank you." I meant it.

"It's been my pleasure. Now, I'm heading home." He paused. "And Lindsay?"

"Yes?"

"Wait until Monday morning to call Peter."

As soon as I could slip away from the real-estate office on Monday, I flew home, settled at my desk/ kitchen table, and nervously dialed Peter's number. My first thought was how young he sounded. He was cautiously polite as he questioned me about No Pudge!. Unlike my experience at my first SCORE appointment, this time I had the answers.

"I'm impressed." he said. "Most start-ups don't have an understanding of margins and pricing and what it costs to get a product to market."

Thank you, Bob and Jay.

"If you'd like to come down, I'll show you around and we can talk details. I'm sure your goal is to get product on the shelf for baking season in the fall."

S*ounds good to me.*

Suddenly he sounded less like a kid and more like someone who knew exactly what he was talking about. "Why don't you fax me your NDA."

My what?

"Once that's signed," he continued, "you can fax your formula and I'll price it. What quantity is it in?"

I couldn't fax my "NDA" because I had no clue what an "NDA" was. And, minor detail, my "formula" was a recipe. This had been going so well. . . . I took a deep breath.

"I'm sorry, Peter — I don't know what 'NDA' means." I hesitated slightly before throwing myself completely under the bus. "And my formula's in small quantities." *Like one pan at a time. . .*

"An NDA is a Non-Disclosure Agreement." His voice was kind. "It's for your protection and it states that I can't use or share your formula."

I suddenly remembered Bob and Jay talking about it.

"And don't worry about the small quantities; my lab can convert it to a manufacturing formula." I could hear the click of calculator buttons being pushed at a furious rate. "We could do a two-hundred-pound run every couple of weeks to start and increase frequency as you grow."

Two hundred pounds*?! How many bags is that?* "Sounds great." *Shit.*

The following week I drove three hours to Brockton, Massachusetts, to meet Peter. Inside the main entrance of the very large, two-story building, the atmosphere was very "big company." I was given a badge with "VISITOR" in big red letters. The receptionist informed me that Mr. Neville would be right out.

"Lindsay?" I turned to a tall, thirty-something, good-looking guy in a pressed button-down shirt and equally pressed khakis. He offered a smile and a firm handshake and escorted me down a long, wide corridor. The place had an echoing, not-enough-furniture feel.

"My father started Concord Foods in the late sixties," Peter said, "but we've only been in this building a few months. My kids think this is the perfect place to ride their Big Wheels."

We chatted easily as he gave me a tour of the impressive facility. The office area, though sparsely furnished, was bright and comfortable. The plant was enormous, filled with machinery and people in white lab coats and hair nets. Everything was spotless, organized. But what impressed me more was that all the employees greeted Peter by name, and he knew every one of theirs. If No Pudge! was manufactured there, I'd be in good hands.

I practically floated out of the parking lot and merged into the traffic flow that would carry me north through Boston and on to New Hampshire. Find a co-packer? Done.

I may not have been getting the support I craved at home, but outside of those four walls, I had an amazing support system. It had just increased by one. Before the year was out, Peter's father would retire and Peter would take over as president. Throughout the next ten years he would never be too busy to answer questions, offer advice or "just talk." Our relationship grew into one of mutual respect and warm friendship.

I was incorporated, trademarked, labeled, packaged, co-packed, "business-carded," and almost ready for lift-off.

Chapter 9

"Lindsay, have you heard of the Fancy Food Shows?"

I was sitting in the SCORE conference room on a gorgeous mid-June day, having just reported to an ecstatic Jay and Bob the details of my visit to Concord Foods. I shook my head. "Fancy Food"? Through the open windows I could hear kids playing in the park across the street.

"The National Association for the Specialty Food Trade puts on two shows a year that showcase specialty foods," Bob explained.

"The New York show is *the* show of the year," Jay chimed in. "Everyone who's anyone in the industry will be there."

Bob leaned towards me. "We think you should go and see what this industry is all about."

New York?! I forced myself to behave like a grown-up, but inside I was jumping up and down like a little girl who had just been told she was going to Disney World. *I'm going to New York! My first business trip!* For a moment I didn't feel like the wife of Paul and the mother of Adam and A.J. — I felt like a "businesswoman." And it felt way cool.

Two weeks later, I boarded a plane in Manchester, New Hampshire. My assignment from Bob and Jay was to walk the show aisles looking for distributors and stores that might be open to eventually carrying the brownie mix, and also for any product that would be competition for No Pudge!. I was traveling with Paul, who spent part of every week in New York City. He'd arranged his schedule so I could share his hotel room, saving precious dollars. The next day I'd fly back on my own. I wasn't going to admit it, but I was grateful for the experienced travel companion. I hadn't been to New York City in years and had never been there alone.

We went directly to the hotel in Midtown and dropped off our suitcases. Agreeing to meet back at the end of the day, we went our separate ways. I grabbed a cab and headed for the Jacob Javits Center.

Twenty minutes later, the cab pulled up to a building that covered four city blocks. A giant marquee read "Welcome NASFT Fancy Food Show." People moved purposefully, intent on whatever awaited them inside this monster of a building. I paid the cabbie and walked behind a group through one of the main doors.

In the cavernous lobby I stopped dead in my tracks. Signs with arrows pointed in every direction. I followed the sign to Attendee Registration.

The lady at the desk smiled. "Company name?"

I don't really have a company yet. I mean I have a business card and it says I have a company — it even says I'm president, if you can believe that — but I don't actually have a product yet. But I will. Soon. "Uh, No Pudge! Foods."

"Lindsay?" She handed me a badge on a long elastic necklace.

NO PUDGE! FOODS, INC.
LINDSAY H FRUCCI
PRESIDENT

Whoa. I hung the badge around my neck. "Could you tell me how to get to the exhibits?"

She silently nodded towards a huge banner to my right. On it was the single word "Exhibits." An enormous arrow pointed to the escalator below.

Duh.

As the escalator made its descent, the noise level increased. When I stepped off, a security guard scanned my badge and waved me through to an enormous hall.

Oh. My. GOD.

I cautiously ventured down an aisle into a moving tapestry of colors, smells, and people. It was like a carnival midway. Booth after booth of every size, shape, and design, all with one common denominator: *food.*

What kind of food, you ask? Chocolate — every kind, color, and shape, plus anything that could be coated in chocolate (chocolate-covered jalapenos, anyone?), salad dressings, dipping oils, chips, candy, bread, muffins, cookies, spring water, mineral water, sparkling water, flavored water, drinks with fizz, drinks without fizz, ostrich, buffalo, bacon, cheese, pickles, cold cuts, mac 'n' cheese, imported pasta, local homemade pasta, pasta sauce, pizza, cereal, popcorn, pretzels. Chinese food, Korean food, Japanese food, Italian food, Polish food, Israeli food, English food (who knew?), German food, Kosher food. Wine. And every booth was offering samples.

Getting hungry? Sound like a wonderful dream? "Bring me chocolate truffles! I need pizza! With smoked salmon! Buffalo, I must have buffalo!" I sampled anything and everything. For about fifteen minutes. *Oy, my stomach. Is there a booth that serves Pepto-Bismol?*

Like to eat and people-watch? Get yourself a badge to a Fancy Food Show. Every aisle was jammed — and I mean *jammed* — with old people in wheelchairs, young people with nose studs and tattoos, men and women in suits, some cruising alone and others followed dutifully by their entourage.

The people manning the booths were dressed in logos: shirts, hats, aprons, chef's jackets, and in one case, fig leaves. (Yes, fig leaves. Gorgeous girl, gorgeous guy, their critical parts barely covered by teeny costumes made from fig leaves. No one was paying much attention to the food they were offering. . . .) Like carnival hawkers, these logo'd beings did everything possible to draw attendees to their booths.

And the smells! The smell of cooking meats mingled with ethnic food mingled with sweet and savory baking. The result? A surprisingly pleasant, yet indefinable olfactory treat.

This was the 1995 New York Fancy Food Show and I was completely overwhelmed.

A couple of weeks before the New York trip, in a what-the-hell moment of sheer bravado, I'd called Bread & Circus to see what it took to get into their stores. The one and only chain of natural food supermarkets in New England, owned by little-known Whole Foods, Bread & Circus was the place for buying — and selling — natural food products. These were the "big boys." But I was having one of those might-as-well-shoot-for-the-stars kind of days, so I called.

The guy on the phone politely explained they couldn't consider a new product until The Big Kahuna had approved it. (Of course he used the man's name, but I think The Big Kahuna fits better.) Suffice it to say, anyone who had anything to do with natural foods and Whole Foods Markets in the nineties knows exactly who I'm talking about. If you wanted your natural product on the shelves of Bread & Circus (which of course you did) you had to get in to see The Big Kahuna. Get in to see him? If you were Nicky New Guy and he didn't know your name, your company, or your product, getting a return phone call, let alone an audience, was a pipe dream. Not that you could blame him. The Big Kahuna was in high demand. I had left at least three messages in the past two weeks.

I'd never met The Big Kahuna, didn't know anyone who had, and had never seen a picture of him. I was in the biggest damn convention center I'd ever seen, walking down one of at least a hundred aisles on one of two floors of at least a hundred aisles each and every aisle was wall-to-wall people. A guy with a dark, full beard passed by, going in the opposite direction, and out of the corner of my eye I thought I caught the name "Kahuna" on his badge. *Could it be?!* I wasn't sure and the crush of people was carrying me further away by the second. *I need to see that badge again!* I took off down the aisle like a running back headed for the end zone in the last seconds of a tied Super Bowl. At the end of the aisle, I tore around the corner and started pushing and shoving my way back up the adjacent aisle, hoping he was moving slowly enough that I could walk past him again. I got to the beginning of the original aisle (you following me here? I've run around the block) and started back down, furiously scanning the crowd.

There! Just ahead I saw him, walking slowly, deep in conversation with another guy. Staring intently at the poor man's chest the entire time, I walked by as closely as I could without knocking him over. *It's him! It's The Big Kahuna!* Without thinking twice, I whipped around and tackled him to the floor. *Uh no, not really. Taking the football thing a bit too far. . .* I whipped around, caught up to them and planted myself directly in their path. Suddenly people had to detour around us, casting annoyed looks as our little threesome came to a grinding halt in the middle of the aisle.

"Excuse me. I'm really sorry to bother you, but I was walking by and noticed your name tag. My name is Lindsay Frucci and I've left a few messages for you over the past two weeks." I grabbed a quick breath and plowed on. "I have a company by the name of No Pudge! Foods, and I'm about to introduce an all natural, just-add-yogurt, fat-free brownie mix that I would love to get into your stores."

At this point his buddy was smiling broadly. The Big Kahuna was not.

Uh oh. "I'd really like to be able to set up an appointment to see you. They're really good and there's nothing else like them." *He doesn't look amused. . . .*

His sidekick, who was looking extremely amused, gave him a nudge. "Anyone with this much chutzpah deserves some help."

But The Big Kahuna just stood there looking at me like I was a crazy person.

Oh shit. What have I done?

After an eternity of seconds, he seemed to decide that I didn't appear dangerous and that maybe his friend was right, I was more brazen than insane. His face softened and he smiled. Sort of.

"Here's what I'll do." He pulled a business card out of his pocket. "Call my secretary and ask her to fax — you do have a fax? Good. Ask her to fax you the list of stores with each store manager's name on it. I'm not going to tell them they have to stock it, but you can tell them I've approved it. Whether or not they carry it is up to them. And you."

"With your attitude," the other guy said, "I have no doubt you'll get your product in the stores."

The Big Kahuna was ready to move on. "Do you have a card?"

I quickly handed him my card.

He glanced down at it. "Good luck, Lindsay. I'll be on the lookout for your product."

In less than sixty seconds it was over. They walked on. I stood there grinning like a fool.

The door hadn't been opened wide, but it had been cracked. As the years went by I realized a crack was enough. You cracked a door for me, in all likelihood I was gonna blow it wide open.

When I met Paul back at the hotel I chattered on about the details of my afternoon, still too wired to notice his lack of response. On our way to dinner I realized he was stonily silent.

"Look, I know you don't approve of what I'm doing," I said. "I know you don't think I can pull this off, but I'm gonna surprise you."

His cold response was a less-than-perfect ending to my wonderful day.

"You pull this off, we'll both be surprised."

At this moment I hate you. "You're wrong. I won't be surprised at all."

It was a quiet dinner.

Chapter 10

A week later, interrupted by "You're kidding?" and "Lindsay, you didn't!" I told Bob and Jay the story of my not-so-chance meeting with The Big Kahuna. As Bob wiped tears of laughter from his eyes, the stark difference between their reaction and Paul's made my heart ache. I offered up a quick, silent prayer. *Thank you, God, for bringing these two men into my life.*

Happy sounds from the park drifted through the open windows. The ache began to melt, a sense of belonging took its place. I relaxed in my chair.

"Well, Lindsay," Jay leveled his gaze at me, "time to sell some brownie mix."

I straightened in my chair. *Hey God — do you think you could have sent me guys who didn't expect quite so much?* "You think I'm ready?"

Jay sighed and looked over his glasses. "Let's review." He wasn't going to let me off the hook. "You're satisfied

Peter's got the formula right?" His eyes were locked onto mine — there was no escape.

I managed an intelligent-sounding "Uh huh."

"And he's ready once you give him the go-ahead?"

I was beginning to feel a little, shall we say . . . foolish? Sure, let's say foolish. I knew all this but was just being irrationally insecure, and Jay had no patience for my insecurities. He and Bob believed I could do anything I set my mind to and believed I was ready to sell brownie mix.

"The labels and bags are ordered and your pricing's set, so what's not ready?"

Cut the crap, girl. I unfroze my shoulders and smiled. "I guess it's time to sell some brownie mix."

Jay gave me a satisfied, "atta-girl" smile.

"Why don't you try Cricenti's and the Hanover Co-op?" Bob sent vibes of reassurance across the table. "Bobby Cricenti knows what you're doing and is supportive of small, local businesses. I'd start with him."

The Cricentis owned three independent grocery stores, the largest one right down the street from Adam and A.J.'s school. Being an "oh-god-it's-three-o'clock-what-am-I-making-for-dinner" kind of woman, I was a daily customer and consequently knew Bobby Cricenti, who ran the three stores, well. Bobby was far from intimidating and probably would have been fine with my dropping in, but I called and made an appointment.

On the morning of the meeting I stood in front of my closet of mom-clothes and agonized over what to wear. My wardrobe of T-shirts, shorts, and flip-flops wasn't gonna cut it. Khakis and a blouse that had actually been ironed rather than pulled out of the dryer and shaken seemed right.

I arrived on time, armed with mock-ups of the package (labels had been ordered but hadn't arrived), baked brownies, and a "Jay and Bob–approved" order form. I entered through the main entrance of the store, but instead of grabbing a shopping cart and starting my daily ramble — or run, as it often turned out to be — up and down the aisles, I made my way around the periphery to land at the Courtesy Booth.

"Hi, Lindsay." Yes, the woman at the Courtesy Booth knew my name. She probably knew 80 percent of the townspeople by name. Hard to imagine, huh? The store is now owned by one of the big chains — I wonder if it's still as personal. Somehow I doubt it.

I smiled at her. "Hi, Janice. I have an appointment with Bobby."

Up until now, I hadn't felt the least bit nervous, but as she reached for the phone I suddenly felt awkward and uncomfortable — like the universe was out of kilter. Right place, wrong . . . something. Being in familiar surroundings was supposed to make this first appointment easier, right? Not.

"Through that door." She nodded towards a door marked "Employees Only."

You know how you can see something every day but not really see it? I had been by this door at least a million times but had never given any thought to what was behind it. Trying to look like this was no big deal, I opened the door and stepped through.

Like Alice and her looking glass, when I stepped through that door I wasn't walking into the offices of a local grocery store. I was taking my first real, official, no-turning-back giant step into an unknown world — the world of the grocery industry.

Twenty minutes later (fifteen spent in idle, small-town chit-chat), I walked out with an order for ten cases of mix. Absolutely no selling had been required — I simply showed Bobby the label, and he said something like "I'll take ten cases." I was suddenly oozing with confidence. *That big company and the financial security I keep telling Paul are right around the corner? They really are! I have a great product in adorable packaging that consumers will love. What more do I need?*

I rode my wave of success to the Hanover Co-op a couple of days later and walked away with another ten-case order.

Back across the table from Jay and Bob, I looked down at a cash-flow spreadsheet Bob had put together for August. The big number 20 twinkled up at me from the column "Cases Sold."

I beamed at the two men. "Twenty cases! Pretty cool, huh?"

Bob smiled. "Someday that'll be two hundred cases. Maybe two thousand."

I was having enough trouble wrapping my head around the idea that my No Pudge! Fudge Brownie mix was about to be sold in stores, and people who didn't even know me — not just friends and family who felt obligated — were gonna buy it. Two thousand cases a month? That was truly beyond my comprehension.

Chapter 11

Peace and quiet on a late August morning. For some wonderful reason, I had the house to myself and was basking in the blissful silence when the phone rudely rang.

"Hello?"

"Yeah, hi, Lindsay. It's Peter. How are you?"

Well, I was *basking in blissful silence.* "Good, thanks. Busy." *Liar.*

"Listen, we just finished your first run and your bags look great."

Suddenly I didn't mind that he'd interrupted my blissful basking.

"I have a truck headed to your area tomorrow."

"Awesome! I'll be here but I have to ask — how big a truck?" There were odd details I didn't think about when we bought our old farmhouse in the boonies. Living on a narrow, dead-end dirt road, we didn't have room for a big truck to turn around. Try dealing with a moving-van driver when he pulls into your driveway and realizes the only way he's going to get out is to maneuver his huge truck backwards for about a mile. We couldn't hear what he was saying as we waved goodbye, but we could see his lips moving and the look on his face. That was enough.

"It's a panel truck," Peter said. "Shouldn't be a problem. How many cases do you want?"

"I have orders for twenty cases, so . . . twenty cases?" Passed my logic test.

There was a brief pause and I thought I caught a hint of suppressed laughter. "Uh, don't you think you should take more than that? What about re-orders and new sales?"

Reorders and new sales? Hadn't thought of those. "Yeah, why don't you send thirty?" *Wow. Thirty cases!* I thought it would be weeks before I would need ten extra cases.

"Take fifty," he said. "You're gonna need 'em sooner than you think."

I didn't want to tell Peter I was worried about how I was going to pay for fifty cases. Thanks to Bob and Jay's mentoring, I had played the "businesswoman" part so convincingly, he assumed I'd planned for any lapse between getting paid and paying him. Wrong. My No Pudge! account was funded by real-estate commissions, and for the past several months I'd been dipping in to cover lawyer fees, ingredients, Lee's designs, and the huge cost of stocking bags and labels. Because I'd been spending less time in the real-estate office, outflow far exceeded income and I wouldn't have enough to cover the cost of those cases until I got paid by Cricenti's and the Co-op. If the stores' payments were even a couple of days late, I'd have to ask Paul for a check to cover the balance. Not exactly at the top of my "fun things to do" list.

"Okay, send fifty."

Fifty cases of brownie mix takes up a lot of space. Peter's driver and I stacked them against a wall in the garage and I immediately began to worry about the car running into them, the roof leaking, it being too warm, too cold — you name it. You'd have thought it was puppies out there, not cardboard cartons filled with bags of brownie mix.

After the truck left, I lifted a case from the top and carried it to my office/kitchen to thoroughly examine it. It looked so professional! *NO PUDGE! Original Fudge Brownie Mix* and the UPC code were printed on the side. A brown cardboard carton with printing on the side probably sounds like a big yawn, but it was the first solid, tangible proof I had a company.

I opened the case and carefully pulled out a shiny, white, heavy-duty paper bag dressed front and back with the colorful labels Lee had designed. I turned the bag over and read the paragraph I'd written:

> I AM A BROWNIEHOLIC. I love thick, fudgy, chewy brownies. I hate fat. In my food or on my hips, fat is definitely something I like to live without. So, for myself and all my fellow fat-hating brownieholics, I've created this mix for chewy, fudgy, FAT-FREE brownies. Now that you've discovered the joy of

indulgence without guilt, the wonder of satisfying a craving and still fitting into your jeans, I'd really appreciate it if you'd tell your friends, family, and even the person standing behind you in the check-out line about NO PUDGE! Fudge Brownies. They'll thank you and so will I!!!

Lindsay H. Frucci
Brownieholic & Founder

My signature stared up at me. Suddenly my legs felt weak. I dropped like a stone into the nearest chair. I couldn't believe what I was holding in my hand. All the work of the past months had culminated in this white paper bag with a colorful label and brownie mix inside. *My* brownie mix.

I loaded twenty cases into the back of our Ford Explorer and headed out to do my first deliveries. At Cricenti's, I carried two cases across the parking lot and in the front door. As I marched through the store lugging my two cartons, I felt awkward and conspicuous.

The woman at the courtesy booth looked up as I approached. "Oh, Lindsay, I'm sorry. We don't take deliveries here. You have to go around back to the loading dock." Paying customer? Front door. Delivery woman? Head for the back. I about-faced and carried the cases back to the car. I drove around back to where two large trucks were backed up to a loading dock. A van and SUV were parked to the side with doors open wide, packed to the gills with brown cardboard boxes much like mine. I grabbed two cases, climbed metal stairs to the crowded dock and crossed a cement platform into what appeared to be total chaos. Cartons of all sizes and shapes covered a small, garage-like space lit by the open door. Drivers were rapidly unloading the contents of their trucks onto dollies. Other men moved through the space carrying boxes or clutching paperwork.

A balding, paunchy man appeared out of a tiny glass office and headed purposefully in my direction. A barcode reader hung from his belt like a holster. His Cricenti's polo shirt stretched across an abundant belly. He was carrying a clipboard.

"What's this?" he nodded to the cases in my arms. In this part of the store, there was no first-name welcome, no friendly flicker of recognition; I was just another delivery to be processed, checked off, and stacked somewhere.

"No Pudge! Brownie Mix. I'm delivering ten cases."

"What is it?"

"No Pudge! Fudge Brownie Mix." In choosing such a "fun" name I hadn't thought of what it would sound like when I actually said it out loud in a public place to someone who couldn't care less. "Bobby ordered ten cases." *Take that!*

"Ten cases?" His face registered disbelief. "I don't have room for ten cases." He didn't care if Bobby or the president of the United States had ordered the mix. This was his turf and he had never heard of this ridiculous-sounding stuff.

"I think he planned on sending some to the other stores." Clipboard Guy didn't hear or didn't care. My bet was on the latter.

Scanning one of the cases with the bar-code reader, he heaved a mighty sigh. "Just put 'em over there for now." He nodded to a miniscule piece of floor space and wrote something on his clipboard. "I'll figure out what to do with 'em later. What did you say it was again?"

"Fat-free brownie mix."

He looked at me with a blank expression, then abruptly turned away.

I carefully put my cases on the floor against the wall. After four more trips, all ten cases were stacked neatly together. As I left, I wondered if I would ever see my bags of mix on the shelves or if they would disappear into the black hole of Cricenti's loading dock.

Climbing back into the car, I drove an hour north to the Co-op. Once there, I headed to the back of the store. I wasn't making that mistake again. This time the man who met me at the door had a list and No Pudge! was on it. He grabbed a young guy with a hand-cart, who unloaded the ten cases and then disappeared into the hinterlands of the store. Done.

I got back in the car to drive home, feeling more than a little let down. When I'd gotten up that morning, I'd eagerly anticipated that this would be the day I would see the mix on the shelves for the first time. I hadn't expected I would abandon it in a dark and chaotic place and hand it off to some strange kid. To make matters worse, I'd been to two different grocery stores and hadn't thought to buy anything to feed my family for dinner. As I turned off the highway, I realized I had to go to Cricenti's yet again.

I dragged myself through the store. S*alad stuff and broccoli.* Check. *Chicken legs and thighs.* Check. *Rice of some sort.* I grabbed a box of rice pilaf mix, but instead of heading to the registers I paused. *What the hell.* Turning around, I hung a right into the Baking aisle. Halfway down I came to an abrupt stop. There, on the left, on the top shelf of the brownie mix section, side by side in all their pink-and-white glory, were two bags of No Pudge! Original Fudge Brownie Mix. *Ohmygod.* Behind them, neat rows of bags disappeared into the shelf. I could see my little pig smiling out from each one. I stood there gazing at my bags of brownie mix, grinning like a fool. Even though I had the aisle all to myself, I turned back to my cart feeling very self-conscious and . . . different.

I had come up with an idea and turned that idea into a product that was now sold in grocery stores. The fact that it was in only two stores was inconsequential. I had done it.

Chapter 12

In the food business, grocery store demos are an expensive and time-consuming fact of life. I hated doing demos, but stores demanded them, so I baked samples, hauled them and all sorts of other paraphernalia to the store, stood behind a table, and became invisible. When was the last time you made eye contact with a Demo Dolly? Like I said . . . invisible.

My first demo was at the Co-op. I worked myself into a nervous snit over it. What if I stood there for four hours and no one wanted to try the brownies? What if people tried them but didn't like them? What if people liked them but thought they were too expensive and wouldn't buy them? Whatif-whatif-whatif. Whatifs can make you crazy and I had a serious case of them.

I decided to check in with the grocery manager before unloading the car. I clearly remember carrying cases through Cricenti's only to be told to walk them right out again. This time I would preserve some modicum of dignity before lugging samples, signs, and supplies through the store. I mean whatif I was supposed to enter by the rear door or whatif I had come on the wrong day or whatif I was there too early to set up? I was a whatif mess.

I found the grocery manager chatting with a customer. His eyes lit up when he saw me; he then excused himself and hurried over.

"You made it! Let me show you where to set up." Pausing, he looked down at my empty hands. "Uh, did you bring your stuff?"

Oh Lindsay, you really are your own worst enemy. . . .

I assured him I had everything and then followed him to the front of the store. Behind a large table, covering the entire end of the aisle, was a wall of smiling pink pigs.

To really grasp the significance of this — which I can assure you I didn't at the time — I offer Lesson #1 in Grocery Industry 101.

In grocery store lingo, the space at the end of the aisle is called an "endcap," and an endcap is *primo* grocery store real estate. Companies pay big, big bucks for an endcap display, which is why (you will now notice the next time you go shopping) the endcap usually features a mega-company product like Tide or Tostitos or Betty Crocker. They're the only ones who can afford it. I didn't know all that yet, but I did know that all those happy pigs were hard to miss.

I went out to the car and began lugging everything in — leaving behind the ten extra cases Bob had convinced me to bring "just in case." I had my samples in a large red cooler and figured I'd be lucky to go through half of them, but as I was putting the first samples on a plate people began reaching for them. "What's this?" became "You're kidding?" when I explained what they were eating.

I found myself desperately trying to talk to people and keep the plate full at the same time. The grocery manager kept wandering by, grinning and nodding as the display dwindled.

I was handing a bag of mix to a customer when I looked up and noticed Jay and Bob standing by the magazine rack, beaming like proud papas. I beamed right back and kept passing out samples. Every time there was a lull in the action they came over and tried to talk, but we never had the chance to exchange more than two words before a customer walked up and they had to step back. Finally they left, probably chortling all the way to their cars. No words had been necessary. Our exchanged "beaming" had said it all.

After Jay and Bob left, the grocery manager stopped by, his hands deep in the pockets of his green apron. "That was all ten cases," he said, nodding at the greatly reduced display behind me. "When these last bags are gone we're out." Barely two of the planned four-hour demo had passed.

"Actually, I have another ten cases in my car." *Bob, you brilliant man.*

"Great! Do you have enough baked samples?"

I was surprised to find I was down to my last pan.

"Why don't we bake some in our bakery?" He reached out and grabbed bags from the display.

In forty minutes I had four more pans of samples ready to hand out. Two hours later, there were only ten bags left — just enough to hold our place on the shelf until I could bring more mix the next day — a mere two-hour round-trip drive.

I was packing my stuff in the now-empty cooler when the grocery manager approached. He was smiling from ear to ear. Come to think of it, he'd been smiling like that all day. "That was one of the best demos we've had in a long time. Congratulations."

"Thanks Ed. This was amazing."

"Would you mind if we started bringing the mix in through our distributor?" he asked. "It would save you driving all the way up here every time we need it, and would make it easier for us."

Are you kidding me? Mind? A distributor!

You're probably wondering why I was so excited. Lesson #2 of Grocery Industry 101. (I'm going to keep this simple because I doubt you give a flying fig about the details of how the grocery industry works, but it might make your next trip to the grocery store a little more interesting.) A distributor is a middleman with a big warehouse and lots of big trucks. Distributors buy large quantities from manufacturers, the product is shipped directly to them, and they deliver to stores. The store can place one order with the distributor for multiple products, so everything's delivered at once, and they get only one bill. That's the tip-of-the-iceberg-you-really-don't-want-to-know-any-more-or-it-would-make-you-crazy explanation.

One demo / one distributor. At this rate I figured I'd be national in no time.

I walked away from the Co-op thinking all demos would be that exciting and productive, and headed to my second demo flying on the wings of that experience. I was about to be brought down to earth with a butt-bruising thud. No other demo would ever equal the wonder of that day.

After my first order from Cricenti's and the Co-op, I turned my attention to the list of eight Bread & Circus stores The Big Kahuna's secretary had faxed. I shipped baked brownies and a bag of mix to each store manager via overnight mail and wrote "PERISHABLE" all over the box. For all the poor guy knew, the box contained sardines or Camembert cheese, so he'd open it right away. Who wants sardines or stinky cheese hanging around their office? My hope was he'd be so thrilled to find my amazing fudge brownies, he'd immediately grab his phone and place an order.

Five stores' managers agreed to carry the mix. And each one asked for demos. The demo that followed the one at the Co-op was just outside of Cambridge, Massachusetts, at the largest Bread & Circus. I'd met Michael, the grocery manager, a couple of weeks before. At the time, he'd been polite and genuinely interested in carrying No Pudge!.

As I walked along the front of the store I quickly scanned for the wall of pink pigs at the end of an aisle. Not a smiling pig to be found. The lady at the Courtesy Booth paged Michael, and when he arrived, she nodded in my direction. He looked at me quizzically. He had no idea who I was or why I was standing there.

Was I that forgettable? Granted I *was* almost old enough to be his mother. . . . "I'm Lindsay Frucci? Here to do the No Pudge! demo?"

"Oh yeah." He nodded to the woman in the booth. "Page Sarah."

Whoa. What happened to "please"?

He turned to me. "Sarah's our in-store demo coordinator. She'll show you where to set up." He walked away.

Okay. . .

Unlike Michael, Sarah was charming. "I'll show you where Michael wants you." She started walking away from the front of the store, her long ponytail swinging across her back. "When I saw you were going to be doing a demo this week I decided to try your mix. I just love it." We continued to walk further into the back of the store. "I can't believe it's fat-free!" she said. "Is it new?" Before I could answer, she stopped near the end of an aisle in a back corner of the store. "This is where he wants you."

"Where?" We were standing in the middle of an aisle. I didn't see one smiling piggy.

"Here by the mix." She pointed downward.

I looked and there, on the bottom shelf, was one bag of mix. I assumed there was a row of bags lined up behind it, but since I wasn't lying on my stomach I couldn't tell.

"Oh." I fumbled for what to say next. "My table won't fit here; it'll take up the whole aisle."

"I have a small demo table you can use. I know this isn't the best location, but it's where Michael wants you."

It was going to be a very long — and lonely — four hours.

"Listen, maybe you should talk to Michael," Sarah said. "You did come all this way and I would think the least he could do is let you set up near the front." Her empathy was empowering.

"Yeah, this just doesn't make sense." *Talk to Michael! That's exactly what I'll do.* "And I don't understand why it's not with the other baking mixes."

She nodded. "I have no say in where things go, I'm just the demo coordinator, but I agree with you."

This is probably nothing more than an oversight. If I politely point it out to him, I'm sure he'd be more than happy to move both the demo and the mix. I headed off to look for Michael with Sarah following. He was a couple of aisles over, kneeling on the floor, stacking cans on a shelf.

"Michael?"

He looked up with a "now what?" expression on his face.

"I'm wondering if I can move the demo closer to the front of the store. The whole point of my being here is for people to try the brownies. But they can't try them if I'm hidden in the back corner." I didn't know I was not-so-slowly getting myself into big trouble. My next couple of sentences sealed the deal. "And I'm also wondering if the mix can be moved to the aisle with the other baking mixes. No one's gonna see it where it is now."

Michael rose to his feet, fixed me with a steely stare and spoke slowly. "Let me give you a little tip. You are a very small fish in a very big pond. I decide where the mix goes and where you do your demo. Not you. I suggest you be quiet and do what you came here to do." With a final glare, he got back on his knees and resumed stacking.

I felt the heat of blood rushing into my face. I was stunned. Humiliated. Sick to my stomach. I turned back towards Sarah, who was looking away as if she didn't want to embarrass me further by making eye contact. Or maybe she sensed that if she did, I'd start to cry. We headed back to my corner.

"I am so sorry," she said quietly.

"It's okay. It's not your fault."

"But he didn't need to be so rude."

"No he didn't." *And I'm almost old enough to be his mother! How dare he talk to his mother that way!*

I learned something that day that had nothing to do with little fish and big ponds. There are people who, when given a position of authority, wield their power like a weapon.

Chapter 13

Red and yellow leaves mingled with the cold rain blowing across the yard outside Sue's kitchen. Winter was coming and the trees were being stripped of the last of their summer adornment. *At least it's not snow. Yet.* Sitting with hands wrapped firmly around a mug of just-poured tea, I was doing my best to keep the outside chill at bay. I blew on the steaming liquid and tried to switch gears from weather to work. "I need something with the logo to wear when I do demos."

"You're talking to the right person." Sue lifted the cover off a large pot on the stove and gave the contents a stir. A comforting aroma filled the small kitchen. Sue was a great cook. She was also a smart businesswoman who ran her own promotions business — she could put a logo on anything. And since I had the cutest logo in the world, we were a great match. She was also running a household and dealing with a husband and two sons.

We were almost twins. As in any sisterhood, we commiserated, compared notes, whined, and understood.

She put the lid back on and leaned against the counter. “How about an apron?”

“Good idea!” I took a noisy slurp of the hot tea. “Do you have a cookie or something?” *Working on the winter weight already. This rate I'll be up 100 pounds by spring.* “How much do you think aprons would cost?”

She was rustling around in her cabinet, “I think you should do T-shirts too. Let's go check some catalogs.” She held up a package triumphantly. “I'll bring the cookies.”

The gloomy weather whines were gone and the gears had been switched.

“I'd love to do T-shirts! I'm right behind you.”

Two weeks later I had aprons with the logo embroidered on them and white T-shirts with the logo silkscreened on the left chest. Across the back they read:

No Fat!
No Guilt!
No Pudge!
Fudge Brownies

It was my first frivolous spend, and I loved them. But loving them didn't pay for them. I rationalized their cost by telling myself it was a sound marketing spend. Although Bob and Jay weren't completely on board with my decision to spend the money, they hadn't disagreed with my persuasive marketing rationalization.

On the home front, the daily saga of No Pudge! was not exactly a "hot topic," so I found it easy not to tell Paul about the purchase. Instead, I decided to surprise him.

"Look what I have for you!" I said as I handed him a T-shirt one night after dinner.

"What's this?" he asked.

"A No Pudge! T-shirt. Isn't it cute?"

He looked at me like I had rocks in my head. "You can afford T-shirts?"

Did I really think he'd be tickled and say, "Oh honey, these are simply adorable!"?

Be excited for me! At least look at it! The fact that he was asking a legitimate question didn't enter my mind.

Buying T-shirts and aprons that I didn't really need and couldn't afford added fuel to his "you don't know what you're doing and this is going to cost us money" fire. His focus on getting us back to financial security was *so* intense and narrow that it left little room for the kids or me and certainly no room for the leap of faith I was asking for. Maybe I should have been more understanding of his perspective, but I wanted him to be more understanding of mine.

So we continued to tiptoe around the 800-pound gorilla that had taken up housekeeping in our relationship, each believing it was the other handing out the bananas that were keeping him around.

Winter came whether I was ready or not, and with it snow, Christmas, and the end of 1995. Late one night after Paul and the boys were in bed, I tucked myself into a corner of the couch, an afghan snug over my legs. The fire that had been crackling and popping in the old fieldstone fireplace an hour before was quieting down to a glowing hiss. Around me, the old farmhouse softly creaked and groaned as it worked to keep us warm and safe. With my hands around the warmth of my almost continuous mug of winter tea, I stared into the dying fire.

Christmas had been hectic but wonderful; Santa was more generous than he'd been in a long time. The boys were healthy, happy. Paul and I had grown proficient at avoiding topics that would bring our gorilla running. If not exactly happy, we weren't seriously unhappy — that was a start.

No Pudge! had finished the year with $42,000 in sales. I'd learned more than I thought possible and was busier than I could have imagined. My support system of Bob, Jay, Lee, Peter, and Sue was solid, strong, and smart.

I didn't have a picture in my head of what "successful" looked like, but *Freedom from Worry* was the caption. I couldn't envision how I was going to get there, but I was sure the journey had to be taken, and I wouldn't be traveling alone. I felt blessed, grateful.

Look out 1996 — here I come!

Chapter 14

The year 1996 got off to a snowy start. Dodging frequent storms, I traveled all over New England as the No Pudge! "Demo Dolly," landing at co-ops and natural food stores from Cape Cod to northern Vermont and every Bread & Circus in between.

Day One: baking and prep, Day Two: the killer. Driving hours to the store, setting up, standing there in my snazzy new apron, smiling, answering questions while handing out brownie samples, packing up, and making the long drive home — usually after dark and often in traffic — was exhausting. But it was also exhilarating. Watching the business grow was energizing enough to keep me putting one foot in front of the other.

Bob and Jay were in full-steam-ahead mode, and how to grow No Pudge! was their favorite topic of discussion. My to-do list teetered precariously from the weight of "top-priority" items fighting for top billing; with every top-priority item I managed to knock off, another always sprang to take its place. The next top-priority item was diversity: in order to grow, I needed more than just one item in the No Pudge! line. Bob and Jay thought a family of three little piggies was the perfect number. Who was I to argue?

Different flavors of the brownie mix would make the line feel gourmet and would be the difference between No Pudge! and others on the grocery store shelves. Consumers who didn't always want their chocolate "straight up" would love it.

I came up with Raspberry Fudge Brownie Mix and Cappuccino Fudge Brownie Mix. Both would be fat-free, all-natural, just-add-yogurt mixes like their big brother Original. Did I spend thousands of dollars on focus groups and market research to figure that out? Nah. I thought about what flavors went really well with chocolate. Both raspberry and strawberry immediately came to mind, but something about Strawberry Fudge Brownie Mix didn't sound right, so I went with Raspberry. That was easy. One down.

Cappuccino was a little more involved — but not by much. In 1994, the nearest place to get "fancy coffee" was Boston, almost three hours away. That is, until a savvy couple opened a small bagel shop and café in town. Even in the land of flannel shirts and jeans, people love their coffee. Casey and Barry bet they'd also love cappuccinos and lattes. Suddenly there was a hip place on Main Street to go for a fancied-up morning joe. I've been a latte-drinking fool ever since. But the rage wasn't about lattes, it was about *cappuccino.* Coffee and chocolate go together — and yes, I know, it's called "mocha." But Mocha Fudge Brownie Mix didn't sound anywhere near as hip, sexy, and *new* as Cappuccino Fudge Brownie Mix.

Done and done.

I headed back to the lab — better known as the kitchen in my 200-year old farmhouse. I began to play "Food Scientist" and ended up turning my kitchen into aromatherapy nirvana. The smell of baking chocolate laced with the smoky aroma of dark-roast coffee and sweet raspberry wafted from my oven, making the old kitchen feel even cozier against the cold winter outside.

My Doubting Thomas husband didn't have a sweet tooth in his head. Throw fresh basil, a handful of garlic cloves, aged parmesan cheese, and walnuts in the food processor and you've got his attention, but he had a resistance to sweets and baking that I envied. That is, until I began testing the raspberry brownie mix.

He'd been cloistered behind the closed door of his home office since early morning. (He had a real office in the house with a desk, multi-line phone, fax machine, and computer. I, on the other hand, had the kitchen table, the kitchen phone, and the family computer I shared with the kids. Who says life is fair?) When I heard his office door open, I was up to my elbows in soapsuds, cleaning up my latest "experiment."

Empty coffee mug in hand, he wandered into the kitchen and sniffed appreciatively. "Smells good."

Whoa! Back up there, Bucko. Say what? "Thanks." Head down, I focused on scrubbing an already spotless mixing bowl. "It's the first two versions of the raspberry brownies. They'll be out of the oven in ten minutes if you want to try 'em." *That's right, be cool.*

"Sure."

"I'll bring you a piece of each when they've cooled down."

He refilled his mug and headed back down the hall to his office.

It wasn't much, but I'd take it.

Having a real, live distributor who was placing the mix in real, live stores had quieted his objections, but we still didn't really talk about No Pudge!. He did his best to be home to make dinner when I was doing long-distance demos. And I did my best to arrange my demos on weekdays when he had fewer travel commitments. It wasn't great, but it didn't suck.

No Pudge! was consuming more and more of my non-Mom time, which translated into dwindling income from real-estate commissions, and I knew he wasn't happy about it. I also knew I was damn lucky to have someone to pay the bills and the mortgage. I couldn't have supported a family while starting my business, and I'm in awe of people who do exactly that, taking far greater risks than I did. I justified the burden I was putting on us — both emotionally and financially — because I believed in what I was doing, and because I was stubborn. Being told by Paul that he did not want me to move forward and that, if I did, I would fail, had become my greatest motivation. I was absolutely determined to prove him wrong.

The brownies were selling. People who tried them at the demos were enthusiastic. I was heading in the right direction. But Paul couldn't see that, so we lived with that large gorilla sitting quietly in the shadows, waiting to pounce.

This morning however, our gorilla seemed to be napping, and I intended to take full advantage. Thirty minutes after Paul left the kitchen, I cracked open his office door and set napkins labeled #1 and #2 on his desk. Each had a moist, chewy brownie on it.

The rapid two-finger pecking, his version of typing, abruptly halted and he looked up from his computer. "Why don't you bring 'em out to the kitchen, and I'll get a fresh cup of coffee?" He grabbed his seemingly bottomless mug.

I cleared a space on the island and set the napkins down while he drained the coffee pot into his mug. He picked up the first piece, held it under his nose, and inhaled like he was breathing in the aroma of a fine wine. "Mmm, I can smell the raspberry." He took a bite and chewed, staring intently into space.

How I've ached for this kind of engagement from him. "So?"

"The flavor is more sweet than anything else." He took another bite, nodding as he chewed. "Yeah, I'm getting chocolate, but not a real hit of raspberry — know what I mean?"

I nodded and made a note on Recipe #1.

"What did you think?" he asked.

"I'll tell you when you're finished — I don't want to bias you." I slid the other napkin toward him. "Movin' on." I was enjoying every second of this.

He grinned. "I have to clear my palate." After taking a sip of hot coffee, he reached for #2. "Smells amazing."

He chewed slowly. "The raspberry may be a little too strong. It kind of leaves an aftertaste."

I picked up my pen and made a note on Recipe #2.

"How'd I do?"

"You did great." I felt a warm flush of happiness rise in my cheeks. Lowering my head, I briskly wiped crumbs from the counter. "All right, guess I'd better get back to my baking. I want to get two more pans done before I have to get the kids."

He started toward his office. "Let me know when they're done and I'll be happy to give you my expert opinion."

"Great." I stopped wiping and watched him walk away. "Frooch?"

"Yeah?" He turned to look at me.

"Thank you."

He smiled slightly. "No problem." Then he turned back and continued to his office.

I stood still until I heard the office door close then took a deep, shaky breath and reached for my two mixing bowls. You have just had a glimpse of the old pre-broke, pre–No Pudge! Lindsay and Paul. Comfortable, smiling, agreeing, in sync. I'd almost forgotten what it felt like. It was like finding an old sweater in the back of your closet that you thought you'd lost. You pull it on, and it feels warm, and comforting, and familiar, and just plain nice. I had trouble seeing the recipes because my eyes were filled with tears. I missed him. I missed us. *Damn, damn, damn.* I wiped my eyes with my back of my sleeve and took one more deep breath.

Chapter 15

On a Wednesday morning in February, I pulled up in front of a snow bank that almost — but not quite — hid a large No Parking sign. Throughout January, we'd been hit by several "small" storms that had each dumped a mere twelve to eighteen inches of the cold white stuff on us. In "Live, Freeze, and Die" New Hampshire (the state motto is actually "Live Free or Die"), snowstorms don't cause a big commotion. Plows just push the snow to the side and we hardy residents continue on about our business. But February had arrived and the snow had continued to fall. Roads, sidewalks, and parking lots were getting smaller, hemmed in by huge snow banks. Hence the almost — but not quite — buried sign.

I hopped out of the car, glanced at the No Parking sign and completely ignored it — such a rebel. Lifting the tailgate, I grabbed the shoulder strap of a beat-up L.L.Bean ski bag. It was stuffed with ski boots, hat, gloves, goggles, two pairs of mittens, extra socks, Chapstick, sunscreen, hand warmers, foot warmers, a baseball cap, and a twenty-dollar bill — the bare essentials for a day at the slopes. Swinging the bag over my shoulder, I staggered, steadied myself, and reached back to haul out a large red cooler. Just in case anyone official was paying attention, which I seriously doubted, I left the tailgate open and headed for the heavy double doors of Mount Sunapee Resort's ski lodge, my ski bag bouncing heavily against my butt with every step.

I headed for a picnic table in a large alcove, where a group of parents were getting ready for a free day of skiing — a privilege we were granted in return for chaperoning our kids on Wednesday afternoons, when they came to the mountain to ski.

Greetings of "What ya got there?" and "Did you bring us brownies?" rose from the few early birds already setting up camp.

"As a matter of fact, I did." I was becoming known around town as the "Brownie Lady" — as in "Hey, it's the Brownie Lady." Kind of weird, but also kind of nice. People in my little town were starting to take my blooming business sort of seriously.

I placed the cooler on one of the tables, dropped my ski bag to the floor with a resounding thud, and rubbed my indented shoulder. "You guys are gonna be my guinea pigs." I pulled my hat more firmly down over my ears and headed back outside.

I moved the car to a less rebellious parking spot, hoisted my skis on my overworked shoulder, and hiked back to the lodge accompanied by the squeaky crunch of my boots on the packed snow. I took a deep breath of icy air, and all the little hairs in my nose immediately stuck together. Yup, it was cold, but it was a crystal-clear, blue-sky, white-world kind of New Hampshire day — and it was mine. I wasn't driving for hours to stand in a grocery store aisle, and I wasn't sitting in my "office" with the phone pinned to my ear. I smiled in pure anticipatory delight. It was going to be a great day.

Bundled up so no skin was left uncovered, I hunkered down for the cold ride up the lift with the rest of the parents, then unfolded and soared down the mountain. Because it was a weekday, there were no lift lines, and we went right back onto the chairlift and repeated the whole wonderful process. Over and over. At 11:30 we tromped into the lodge for a quick lunch and leg rest before the busloads of kiddos arrived at 12:30 and chaos ensued.

I stood next to the picnic table, opened the large red cooler and pulled out plastic-wrapped plates of brownies. Behind each plate I placed hand-lettered signs that read either "Cappuccino" or "Raspberry." In the center of the table, I stacked a bunch of fill-in-the-blanks questionnaires for evaluating each batch.

Hands immediately started reaching for brownies. "Eat dessert first" seemed to be the motto of this crowd. As I headed towards the cafeteria line for my usual cheeseburger, fries and hot chocolate, I could hear "Ooh, raspberry!" and "This is fun!" Yeah, this *was* fun. By the time the kids arrived, there was nothing left but empty plates and full questionnaires. Just like Paul and my carpenters, this group took their responsibilities of taste-testing seriously.

That afternoon I sat in the car while A.J. said goodbye to his friends, and read through the results. I was in complete agreement with the clear favorite in each category. Original now had a couple of siblings, Raspberry Fudge Brownie Mix and Cappuccino Fudge Brownie Mix. No Pudge! was a family. Just like real kids, getting them ready for the world was going to cost money, and I was running frighteningly low. The time had come to go to the bank.

Over the next nine years I ran head-long into two kinds of bankers — the open-minded, creative, think-outside-the-box kind, and the exact polar opposite — closed-minded, rigid, and (in my humble opinion) sexist. Scott, the vice president at the local bank that had given Paul and me a mortgage when no one else would, was one of the good guys and therefore the target of my plan to get my first 2,500-dollar line of credit.

A quick aside to explain why I have the impression of bankers that I do: At about year eight, I needed a 50,000-dollar line of credit and approached a large New England bank that marketed itself as reaching out to, and supporting, women-owned businesses. When I called to make an appointment, the man I was connected to asked a couple of brief questions and told me to send my financials. No, I didn't need to come down to meet him yet, just send the numbers and he would get back to me quickly. By that time I was a firm believer in face-to-face meetings when you wanted to get something important accomplished, but I reluctantly agreed and sent the financials via overnight mail.

After a week, I called and left a voice mail. It was another week before he returned my call, and then he proceeded to tell me — in a very short and dismissive way — that they wouldn't loan me money because my company was insolvent.

Excuse me? For seven straight years No Pudge! had experienced double-digit growth in an extremely expensive, competitive industry. We were profitable, but we needed the line of credit to help with cash flow as we underwent a successful national-distribution expansion.

I was stunned speechless. Then absolutely livid. I considered storming his office and stuffing the loan papers up his nose, but that would have been a selfish indulgence, and I was way beyond that. Reality? I didn't have the time or emotional energy to do more than imagine how satisfying that would have been.

I got my 50,000-dollar line easily from a local bank, one of the good guys. One year later, that same, big bank called and offered a completely unsolicited, pre-approved 100,000-dollar line of credit. No paperwork required. After checking out my company, they decided we looked so promising that they wanted to help. I took them up on their offer and never used it. But taking it felt like the equivalent of Julia Roberts flaunting her classy, dressed-to-the-hilt self to those bitchy sales clerks in "Pretty Woman" and saying "Mistake. BIG mistake."

Back to Scott, our local good-guy banker. I arrived at the bank and was ushered into his small office. Tall, dark-haired, and younger than me by at least ten years, he rose from his chair with a big smile. Behind him, the top of his credenza was covered with half a dozen mismatched frames holding pictures of kids and dogs. I'd been in his office many times before, always to talk real estate, never as the president of No Pudge!. For the next five minutes, we engaged in obligatory small talk until he said, "You didn't come in here to chat. What can I help you with?"

"I need a 2,500-dollar line of credit for No Pudge!."

He steepled his fingers, nodded, and waited.

I pulled my chair close to his desk and opened the manila folder Bob and Jay had helped me prepare; it was filled with financial reports, consumer letters, and local news clippings about me and the brownies. Taking a big breath, I launched into my spiel about No Pudge!'s growth, consumer enthusiasm, the two new flavors, and our growing costs, all the while passing pertinent information across his desk.

He listened, asked a few questions, briefly looked over the information, and then looked up at me. "Will Paul be cosigning this?"

Shit. "I'd rather he didn't. I'd really like to do this on my own."

He raised his eyebrows. "That's going to be a tougher sell. We have our weekly loan meeting on Friday morning — let me see what I can do. I'll call you when I know." He studied me. "If they don't go for this, will Paul cosign?"

I have no idea and don't want to have to ask. "Yes." *I hope. . .*

Feeling angry, frustrated and demoralized, I walked out of the bank. It was demeaning not to be able to get such a small loan on my own. Of course, Paul did have a good, steady job and made a good, steady income. On the other hand, my income had been dwindling over the last few months and wouldn't be heading in the other direction anytime soon — my tiny start-up company wasn't going to be profitable for a while. Never mind that I had no experience running a business and no experience in the industry my business was in. And, minor detail, we had a bankruptcy in our not-so-distant past. I wasn't exactly a slam-dunk for approval. But it was a small, local bank, they knew me well and . . . and nothing. They were local and I was local and that was about it.

That turned out to be enough. Scott called late Friday morning and told me the committee had discussed my situation at length and decided to give me the loan.

Bob and Jay were ecstatic.

I wasn't sure how I felt. I was taking on debt — something I'd been determined not to do. Happy! Scared. Happy! Scared.

Chapter 16

It was Adam's thirteenth birthday. And I was leaving.

I'm a rotten mother. I hope I made enough brownies. A good mother would be staying home to make her son a birthday cheesecake and his favorite dinner. Did I remember the hotel confirmation? I think he understands — he said he didn't mind waiting till Sunday night to celebrate. I can't believe I'm not going to be home for his birthday. I'm so excited! Maybe we'll get picked up by some huge store and we'll grow really, really fast and I'll make millions and show Paul he was wrong and . . . I'm a rotten mother.

I was on my way to exhibit at my first trade show — the Northern New England Products Trade Show in Portland, Maine. I was absolutely wracked with guilt, but not so wracked that I wasn't in the Explorer, cargo area loaded with everything I could possibly need, picking up my helper-for-the-weekend, Sue.

She popped her one small suitcase in the back and hopped in laughing. "Doesn't look like you forgot anything."

She held her hands in front of the heating vent on the dash. The March sky was threatening rain for the umpteenth day in a row. "How was Adam this morning?" Another mother — knows exactly where my head is at.

"He seems okay. I'm just not sure I am."

"Let it go. You'll make a big deal of it Sunday night, and he'll forget all about your not being there today."

"Yeah, until he needs therapy in twenty years to deal with the trauma of his mother abandoning him on his thirteenth birthday."

"Adam?" Sue laughed. "I don't think you have to worry." She cranked the heat up a notch then looked at me. "Speaking of the men in your life, how's Paul?"

Icy splashes began to hit the windshield. "He's . . . distant. There but not there."

She nodded.

We were quiet for a moment.

"Enough family stuff!" I banged the steering wheel with my hand. "Time to get down to serious matters!" I turned to her with a grin. "Where should we go for dinner tonight?" Lindsay & Sue's Very Big Adventure without Husbands or Kids had begun.

"Good God. This is insane." I muttered. The noise level at the Portland Civic Center was so high that I doubt Sue heard me. We searched for our booth in the cold, echoing arena, carefully picking our way through the maze of wooden crates, open cartons, and packing materials that littered the aisles. Exhibitors, intent on the task at hand, were hammering, hanging banners, placing their wares "just so," then standing back to make sure they looked perfect.

Welcome to trade-show set-up day. This would be the first of what now seems like hundreds of trade shows I did, and it never ceased to amaze me that the morning after set-up, when the show officially opened, all would be orderly, brightly lit, and sparkly clean. The union workers who set up and rip down trade shows pull off seemingly impossible feats at every show. Wouldn't it be nice if you could order them to show up at ten o'clock p.m. on Christmas Day when the house is completely trashed?

"That's it," I said to Sue as we stood facing the back wall of the arena. "This booth number doesn't exist." We were cold, hungry, and frustrated — a dangerous combination that was about to make for two very unhappy, perimenopausal women. If we couldn't find the booth, warm up, and get something to eat quickly, it was gonna get ugly. Ugly.

Out of the corner of my eye I noticed a middle-aged woman intently scribbling on the clipboard in her hands. She was dressed in a University of Maine sweatshirt with a picture of a snarling black bear on the front. I made eye contact with the bear. *Tell me about it.* Then I noticed the badge hanging around the woman's neck. A show official! Bearing (no pun intended) down on the poor woman, with Sue close on my heels, I called out to her. "Excuse me!"

"How can I help?" She gave me a big, dimply smile.

"We can't find our booth." I held out the paper. "It doesn't seem to exist."

I was sure the show people had made a mistake, she was going to be totally surprised and we'll-get-this-straightened-out apologetic, but instead she gushed, "You're a new company with us this year! Wonderful! Welcome!" She pointed behind us to a big sign over a large doorway. We turned around. "FIRST-TIME EXHIBITORS"

She was positively effusive. "Your booth's in that room. And you're lucky — the heat's on in there!" My annoyance deflated like a huge balloon. I felt like an idiot.

"Oh, and ladies?" Another idiot arrow headed in our direction. "I don't know if you've read your welcome packet, but we'll be serving free lunch in the food court area starting in —" she glanced down at her watch "— fifteen minutes. Have a good show!" With a smile and a wave she was off.

Sue started to laugh. "How did we not see that stupid sign?"

We were both laughing as we walked through the door into the warm room where our booth was waiting.

The next morning we were ready a full hour before the show opened, dressed exactly alike in pink turtlenecks, white button-down shirts, and khakis. Over this adorable get-up (hey, it seemed adorable at the time), we wore the white aprons with the No Pudge! logo. Across the back wall of the 10' x 10' booth a large canvas banner read "Brownies without Guilt, Don't You Love It?" and pictured my happy, smiling pig. The long table in the front of the booth was covered with pink-and-white striped fabric. In the middle, easily accessible to anyone walking by, were the all-important baked samples and bags of mix. Stationed behind the table, we'd be able to talk to happily munching customers while replenishing the rapidly disappearing (we hoped) samples from the red coolers underneath. Order forms and information on case size and price were stacked in the corner. We were ready.

When the doors opened at nine, we stood at attention behind our table, anticipating a crowd of excited buyers, all clamoring for the brownies. Nothing. At 9:15 a slow trickle of people started down our aisle, stopping at some booths and barely glancing at others. Thirty minutes later they were five deep in front of our table. Sue and I couldn't keep samples on the plates. Word had gotten out about the fat-free brownies in aisle 15B and we were inundated. People oohed and aahed and said over and over and over that they "couldn't believe" the brownies were fat-free.

By the end of the show, we were out of samples and drop-dead exhausted. No Pudge! Fudge Brownies had been a hit.

Sue and I loaded up the Explorer. We'd written a ton of orders — most for only one or two cases, but the mixes would be in far more stores than before the show. Maybe no big chain had picked them up, but I'd taken a big step towards increasing distribution. We were both too tired to make conversation on the ride home. In her driveway, I pulled her suitcase out of the back and gave her a bear hug.

"Thank you so much. I couldn't have done it without you."

"Are you kidding? I had a blast!" She looked at my tired face and rounded shoulders. "Now go home to your birthday boy."

I took a deep breath. "Yup," I said, climbing back behind the wheel. "That's where I'm going."

I pulled out of her driveway and headed home to a thirteenth birthday celebration.

Chapter 17

"Good morning, No Pudge!." I glanced up at the kitchen clock — yup, still morning. "May I help you?"

"Can you tell me where I can buy No Pudge! Brownie Mix near me?"

I pulled the store list out of the milk crate/filing box at my feet. "Where do you live?" Between my distributor and the new stores I'd picked up at the show, I was confident I'd be able to direct her to a store in her area.

"Waukee, Iowa. It's not far from Des Moines."

Des Moines?? "Umm . . . we're a tiny little company in New Hampshire. We're not in Iowa yet." I paused, dying to know. "Can I ask how you heard about us?"

"My sister's here from Massachusetts. She brought two bags in her suitcase."

She packed my brownie mix in her suitcase!

"Can't you get it into a grocery store near me?" This lady was making me happier and happier.

"I can try, but it might take a while. In the meantime I could send it to you." I never dreamed she'd take me up on my offer. We're talking brownie mix here, not small-vineyard wine from Napa.

"How soon can you get it to me?"

With that phone call, No Pudge! mail order was born. I had no idea what to charge and didn't include the cost of packing materials or my time, but it didn't matter. Word was spreading. The phone began ringing at all hours. I tried ignoring it during dinner, in the evening and on weekends, but I was so excited that people were actually calling that it was almost impossible not to pick up — a fact that didn't make Paul or the kids very happy.

Suddenly, I needed an off-hours receptionist, a customer service department, and an order department. Bob and Jay suggested I hire a call center, which would provide all those and make it look seamless to the outside world. And if I was going to get myself a call center, then it also made sense to get a toll-free number.

Once all this was in place, No Pudge! would appear to be a big company with all the resources necessary to grow and succeed. For all my customers would know, I'd be hanging out in a big corner office — I *was* president and CEO, after all — when in reality, I'd be sitting at the kitchen table in my antique farmhouse in The Boonies, New Hampshire. I ordered the toll free number — 1.888.NOPUDGE — and signed up the call center.

Every morning after I got the kids off to school, the kitchen cleaned, the dogs fed, the beds made, and the first load of laundry started, I'd gather the faxed orders from the call center the night before, settle down at my "desk," and get to work. An exciting turn of events — except that processing and packing the orders took a ton of time away from my primary goal: growing distribution.

I'd also agreed to do demos in a lot of the stores that had placed orders at the show. A couple of days a week I was prepping and doing demos in Vermont, New Hampshire, and Maine — not to mention constant requests from my increasingly demanding biggest customer — Bread & Circus. I had to come to grips with the fact that saying "no" to demo requests — especially when they were far away or repeat performances — was not going to kill my business. I needed to be spending less time traipsing all over New England playing Demo Dolly and more time on the phone, following up on leads.

One such lead was a tip I'd received at the Portland show. The owner of another small food company told me about a distributor located in Long Island that was open to new products and distributed to smaller chains and independents in Connecticut and Metro New York.

Although he was sure his salsa was better than anyone else's, the distributor wasn't so sure they needed to add another salsa to the long list they already carried. I had a distinct advantage — I knew they didn't carry any other fat-free, all-natural, just-add-yogurt brownie mixes. Since I desperately wanted to expand distribution outside of northern New England, they sounded like a fit.

I left a few messages but didn't get any response. Then late one afternoon the boys were settled in the kitchen, not so quietly doing homework, when someone finally called back. I grabbed the phone and headed for my emergency office — a large walk-in broom closet. Closing the door, I settled my derriere precariously on an upended bucket. Sitting in the pitch dark, I explained to the person on the other end of the phone, who turned out to be one of the owners, why I'd been calling.

"Fat-free brownies?" He was polite, but skeptical. "How can they be good if they're fat-free?"

"Let me send you some. I'll even do the baking so all you have to do is open the box and try them." Begging? Nah. In sales it's called "overcoming objections." "Come on, you have nothing to lose." And a bit of begging for good measure.

He laughed. "Send me a couple of bags, I'll have my wife bake one. She's the real test. If she likes them, we'll talk."

A full two weeks passed before I heard back, and when I did, the news was good. His wife loved the brownies. *Yippee!* I did a dance around the kitchen.

But there was a catch. "We have a large booth at the Fancy Food Show in June," he said. "We'd like to introduce them there. The charge for the demo space is only $800."

Only?! For a mere $800, plus airfare, hotel, and meals, I could get twenty-four inches of counter space in their booth and the privilege of standing for three eight-hour days passing out samples. Even if I were extremely frugal (like not eating) it would cost me a minimum of $1,600 — a small fortune. "You've got a deal." I wasn't in a position to argue. I needed this distribution.

That $1,600 would turn out to be an investment even Warren Buffet would be proud of. The pay-off down the road would be — quite simply — huge.

As far as I know, 1996 was the one and only year the Summer Fancy Food Show was held in Philadelphia. Since I wasn't involved in set-up, I flew into Philly late the night before the show opened and arrived at the convention center bright and early the next morning, pulling a portable dolly loaded with coolers of samples. Even with only a few people wandering around, the size and scope of the show was intimidating.

The booth where I'd be spending the next three days was actually four booths put together. My little twenty-four inches of counter space seemed much smaller than I'd imagined (I know, twenty-four inches is twenty-four inches, but I had visualized it as bigger. What can I say — I'm truly numbers-challenged). I barely managed to fit three sample plates and a bag of each flavor on it. The space underneath was too small for even one cooler so I pulled out enough pans to start the day and sent the rest to a walk-in cooler somewhere in the hinterlands off the show floor.

This set-up was not optimal and I was unnerved. I had memories of walking the New York show and being blown away by the hordes filling the aisles. What if I ran out of samples? Whatif I couldn't get anyone to go get more for me, and I had to try to find the off-the-show-floor cooler by myself? Whatif I got lost in the hinterlands? Whatif someone important came by while I was gone? Ah, the old whatifs. One whatif leads to another whatif and another in a lovely example of the snowball effect. You'd think I would have figured out that whatifs rarely happen, but I wasn't there yet. It didn't matter. Soon I was so busy I didn't have time to breathe, let alone worry about what might happen if. . . . The hordes had arrived.

The first day of the Fancy Food Show is always Sunday. Every small gourmet or grocery or catering or anything-having-to-do-with-food business owner comes on Sunday and brings his or her wife, husband, sister, brother, best friend, aunt, uncle, mother, or grandfather. Sunday is essentially an adult-only feeding frenzy. The throngs wander up and down the aisles trying everything from salmon sausage to portabella pizza to raspberry rugalah to fat-free brownies. And at this particular show, it turned out that the masses had two fat-free brownies to try. And they were only an aisle apart.

"Have you tried the fat-free brownies in the next aisle?" I was asked over and over. When I said I hadn't had a chance, I was assured I had nothing to worry about.

"Yours are so much better."

The general consensus was that my brownies were "real" and the others were . . . not? I hoped people weren't just being polite. I made a mental note to investigate the other company but never followed up. For three days I barely took pee breaks.

On day three, as the show was winding down, I squatted behind my counter getting more samples. When I straightened up, three men in dark suits, white shirts, and striped ties were standing in front of the booth waiting for me to reappear.

"Oh!" I was startled by their sudden and very businesslike appearance.

"Sorry." Smiling, friendly. "Didn't mean to startle you."

Okay, who are these guys and what do they want? I fixed the ever-present smile back on my face. My cheeks were starting to hurt from so much damn smiling. "Would you like to try a fat-free brownie?"

They all reached eagerly for a sample. One by one they tried samples of all three flavors while carefully watching one another's reactions.

Who are these guys?

When they finished chewing, one of them, a slender guy with thick, gray hair and mustache smiled and said, "We've been hearing about these the entire show and had to come try them."

"You've been hearing about my brownies?" *Hmm. . .* I suddenly had a feeling I knew who the Three Musketeers were. "So, what do you think?"

"They're very good." He sounded surprised. "I guess we should tell you," he said, lowering his voice and leaning in like he was about to let me in on a deep, dark secret. "We sell fat-free brownies too."

I leaned across the table and whispered, "I kinda figured that out."

Silver Hair laughed heartily, extended his hand, and introduced himself. The other two followed and all handed me their business cards. I caught the company name "Campbell's" but not much more. They chatted a minute longer, wished me luck, and said goodbye. I watched the three dark suits disappear into the crowd.

Campbell's? Damn. Am I in trouble? Then I looked at their cards and almost laughed out loud with relief.

On the card it was clear that Campbell's was the parent company, but the actual brand of the brownies was front and center. It was the fat-free brownie I had dragged the kids out to try, in what seemed like an eternity ago. The one my boys said tasted like raisins. The one made with prune puree. The one that was so awful.

I found myself grinning from ear to ear. "Whatif" you made a brownie with prune puree? I knew the answer to that one. It would taste like raisins and mine would be better. Much better. Putting their cards in the pile with all the rest, I turned to talk with another person who had appeared at the booth. So much for the competition.

In three long days, I talked with and fed samples to about a gazillion people. One bright spot was an adorable young woman with beautiful strawberry blonde waves and a hundred-watt smile. Robin worked for another New Hampshire baking-mix company. She gave me her card and told me not to hesitate to call if I had any questions about the business or simply needed someone to vent to.

By the time the show was over, my head was spinning. I packed my stuff into my trusty red coolers and dragged them and my weary butt to the airport. When I crawled into bed that night it was actually the next morning. For five short hours I slept the flat-out sleep of the wiped-out entrepreneur. Then the boys were up and Paul was up, and it was time to get ready for school. A new day had begun after a short night that, thanks to late flights and delayed flights and cancelled flights and don't forget lost luggage, I would relive — much like Bill Murray in the movie Groundhog Day — over and over and over.

One month later, on a sunny, late-July afternoon, the phone rang and my $1,600 trade-show investment began its journey.

"Good afternoon, No Pudge!. May I help you?"

"May I please speak with Lindsay?" A soft male voice, very precise in its articulation.

"This is she."

"Lindsay, my name is Santiago Uranga from the H. E. Witt Company in Los Angeles. I doubt if you remember me, but we met in Philadelphia at the Fancy Food Show."

Amazingly, I did remember him. Vividly. I hadn't known I remembered him until I heard his voice, but now I could picture him perfectly: a slender, balding, not too tall, Hispanic gentleman in glasses and an impeccable gray suit. Polite, friendly, he'd loved the brownies. Just like dozens of others. But something about him had struck a chord. Karma? Maybe. The universe working its wondrous magic? Maybe that too. The bizarre workings of an overextended and exhausted mind? Yeah — that could be it.

After we exchanged pleasantries, he said, "I'm a broker in southern California and one of my largest accounts is Trader Joe's. I'd love the opportunity to present your brownie mix to them."

This was 1996. I'd never heard of them.

"I'm not familiar with Trader Joe's."

If Santiago was stunned that someone who owned a food company wasn't "familiar" with Trader Joe's, he hid it beautifully. Trader Joe's, he explained, was based in Pasadena, California, had about 100 stores on the West Coast, and was getting ready to embark on an East Coast expansion.

"They're a very unique chain with a very loyal customer base," he said. "Much of what they sell, you'd never find at the big chain stores, and they don't use distributors. They buy direct from the manufacturer in large quantities to keep prices low."

The truth was, their customer base went far beyond loyal. Trader Joe's enjoyed a fanatic, almost cult-like following on the West Coast, and the phenomenon was about to spread across the country. But I was cautious about dealing with a broker and this discount-sounding chain. I asked Santiago to send me information about his company and said I'd get back to him.

The next morning I placed my first of many calls to Robin. *God, please let her remember me, or else this is gonna be real embarrassing.*

Her voice was cheerful and upbeat and full of recognition.

I told her about Santiago and my conversation with him.

"They're a great chain," she said. "If I were you, I'd give it a shot."

That was all I needed.

I called Santiago that afternoon. The road ahead seemed bright and sunny and filled with limitless opportunities.

Unfortunately my personal barometer wasn't picking up the hurricane that loomed just over the horizon.

Chapter 18

My mother passed away suddenly and unexpectedly when I was twenty-one. A few years after she died, my father married a lovely Southern lady and moved to her home on the banks of the Pagan River in Smithfield, Virginia. My first impression of Helen was that she was a superficial Southern Belle - all sugar and spice sweetness. It didn't take long for me to realize how wrong I was. Beneath that sweet outer shell was a core of pure iron. She was a true Steel Magnolia and I absolutely adored her. In return, she loved her late-in-life adopted family as completely as if we were her own.

A petite, silver-haired beauty who believed a lady was never seen — by anyone — without her make-up, Helen Boswell Ames Head had a passion for golf and bridge and played regularly until she was eighty. Her weaknesses were desserts of any kind, good scotch, and my husband. She thought Paul walked on water and could do no wrong. He was crazy about her, too, and happily waited on her hand and foot. She believed deeply in the values with which she had been raised — to behave like a lady no matter the circumstances and to hold on to your pride and dignity, no matter the cost.

On the surface, my father seemed to be her perfect match. As a younger man he had been rakishly handsome with black hair, a narrow, well-trimmed mustache, and deep brown eyes. Although his hair had grayed and thinned and the deep brown eyes had faded with age, he was still handsome. He was an accomplished artist. The steep mountains and rugged coastline of northern New England and the delicate beauty of the Tidewater Virginia marshes, two distinctly different places he had called home, were his favorite subjects. In his later years, his work brought him both acclaim within the fine-arts community and a small but steady income.

To the outside world my father was dapper and charming. But with his family he had a quick, judgmental temper and a self-obsessed focus — character traits that didn't mellow with age. Demanding and selfish, he could be downright nasty when things didn't go his way.

To get relief from the hot, muggy Tidewater Virginia summers, Dad and Helen rented a house near us every year — arriving in June and staying through the end of August. The last two summers had been increasingly difficult as my father became more and more cantankerous. A series of mini-strokes in the spring of 1996, leaving him weakened on his right side and in need of a walker to get around, did nothing to help his disposition.

He was left-handed so still able to paint, and his painting was the only thing that kept him tolerable. We all shuddered at the thought of a stroke — no matter how mild — that would render him unable to put brush to canvas.

Dad and Helen had dinner with us three or four nights a week. During the day I spent as much time as my crazy kid/home/work schedule allowed, helping Helen care for him, but still she took the brunt of his mood swings. She handled the burden with grace, but by the time they left in August, she was completely exhausted. I hated to see her leave and worried she wouldn't be able to handle him without my help, but watching their car pull out of the driveway I felt a guilty — almost giddy — relief. That relief was short-lived.

It was hurricane season in the Atlantic, and Hurricane Fran was forming in the Caribbean. One scenario had it heading straight for the Mid-Atlantic coast. I watched the news every night for the current prediction, but was so wrapped up in house, kids, and No Pudge! that I didn't spend a lot of time thinking about it. After all, I assured myself, Helen had lived in that house forever, and they had plenty of friends to check up on them.

Summer was over, the kids were getting settled back in school and I was once again focused on moving forward on my journey. On the No Pudge! front, Santiago and I were working to get all the paperwork together for Trader Joe's. He was as meticulous with his paperwork as he was with his appearance, and I knew what we submitted would be perfect. The mail-order business was slowly increasing, and I'd hired a part-time bookkeeper. I was still showing the occasional house to the occasional buyer, but doing my best to keep it to a minimum.

About a week after Dad and Helen left for Virginia, Paul and I were getting ready to enjoy a few quiet, post-dinner minutes together. Both boys had erupted from the table as soon as they swallowed their last bites and headed for the door. "Excuse me," I said to their retreating backs. "Aren't you forgetting something?"

Busted.

"Oh yeah. Sorry." They headed back to the table to clear their plates. I shook my head. Would they ever do it without being reminded? At eleven and thirteen, they weren't there yet. I picked up my glass of wine and was just settling back in my chair when the phone rang.

"I'll get it!" yelled A.J. from about six feet away.

I cringed. "You don't need to yell. We're not deaf."

He picked up the phone. "Oh hi, Bumpa."

I locked eyes with Paul and groaned quietly. *Nononono.*

"Here she is. Bye, Bumpa." A.J. handed me the phone and disappeared.

"Helen's in the hospital." He sounded alone and a little helpless.

"What happened?"

"She's been having a lot of pain in her back. Bettie took her to the doctor this morning and he admitted her to the hospital. They told her she'd be there for a few days. Maybe Bettie could tell you more."

"Are you alone?"

"Of course I'm alone," he snapped. "Who did you think would be here? I am perfectly capable of taking care of myself."

So much for alone and helpless.

"Yes, Dad, I know you are." I closed my eyes. I was too tired for a tirade tonight. "What's the weather forecast saying? Any news on the hurricane?" Moving right along. . .

"It's supposed to hit tomorrow night. Looks like we're just north of the eye."

"Then I'm flying down tomorrow." *Did I really just say that? Out loud?*

"You don't need to do that." His protest was weak, and I didn't blame him. He needed a walker to get around and under the best of circumstances it was probably not a good idea for him to be alone. Especially with a hurricane coming.

"If I stay here I'll just worry about you."

"Well, I'm sure Bettie and David wouldn't mind picking you up at the airport." He wasn't going to admit it, but I could hear the relief in his voice. "Do you have their number?"

Although I'd never met them, I knew that Bettie and David Olsen had practically adopted my father and Helen, who were twenty years their senior. At first, the friendship had been predominantly social, but as my father and Helen aged, Bettie began taking Helen shopping and to get her hair done, and David came by to fix things around the house. I had no intention of asking them to pick me up at the airport, but thought I should let them know I was coming.

I made my reservations for an early-morning flight and then called. Bettie explained that Helen's pain was due to a worsening of the osteoporosis in her spine. She was also suffering from exhaustion. Part of the reason she'd been hospitalized was to give her a break from the situation at home.

"They need help, Lindsay." Bettie said. "We're happy to do what we can, but they need someone there all the time. Helen won't let me call Wilson and Cindy, so they don't know how bad things have gotten." Helen's Steel Magnolia pride made it hard for her to tell her son and daughter-in-law that all was not happy at home.

That was about to change.

My white-knuckle, rollercoaster flight on a small commuter plane, a few hours ahead of a major hurricane, was enough to make me want to get down on my knees and kiss the ground when we landed. Bettie and David had insisted on picking me up. The first time they laid eyes on me, I was the color of peas. Bettie took one look and then enveloped me in a big hug. David was right behind her. For the next four hellish days, they were the only bright light in a dark and gloomy world.

As predicted, Hurricane Fran arrived overnight. Although the main force of the storm made landfall on the North Carolina coast, Tidewater Virginia was hit with strong winds and heavy, driving rain. We lost power and the yard was littered with tree branches, but the solid little house on the Pagan River survived the storm.

The days passed way too slowly, held together by the glue of almost constant arguing with my father. *You're an adult!* I kept telling myself. *Don't let him talk to you like that!* But being alone with him in such a concentrated environment made it hard to not slip back to being his little girl — which, contrary to the image conjured by the phrase "Daddy's little girl," was not a happy place for me.

I spent as much time as possible at Helen's bedside. I was determined to convince her that she could no longer manage the situation at home by herself. She was a smart woman, but knowing she had reached a point of needing help, and actually asking for it, were two very different things. Finally, she reluctantly gave me permission to talk to Wilson and Cindy. They immediately said they'd hire a full-time housekeeper.

"We don't need some stranger in here," my father growled, gripping the bars of his walker and struggling to straighten up. "We can take care of ourselves."

"No, Dad, you can't." *Patience, Lindsay. Patience.* "Helen's in pain. She can't drive, cook, or clean. And you can't take care of her and the house. Please don't make this harder than it already is."

But he was going to make damn sure I knew he didn't like it. I tried to be understanding of the fact that these unavoidable changes to his world must be very difficult, but his short-tempered, argumentative behavior made compassion really hard.

Another fun issue? He insisted he could still drive. The very idea had me reaching for a paper bag to breathe into. His being eighty-three years old was just the tip of the iceberg. He needed a walker to get around, he had weakness on his right side, and his reflexes were shot.

"I know this is hard, but you need to think realistically. If a little kid ran into the street in front of you, do you really think you could stop in time?"

He thought for about a minute, and then stubbornly insisted he could still drive. I tried to be empathetic. I tried hard, then hid the car keys. He'd be furious, but I'd be safely back in New Hampshire before he realized what I'd done. Yes, I was a coward. And I had absolutely no problem with that.

The day before Helen came home from the hospital, Bettie and David were waiting in the driveway to take me to the airport.

The power was back on, the yard was cleaned up, the refrigerator was stocked, and the car keys were hidden. My father and I stood facing each other on the screened-in porch, my packed suitcase on the floor beside me.

"Bye, Dad." I reached over and gave him a big hug. He was a pain in the ass, but he was my dad, and I was worried about him. When I pulled away, I was startled by the tears in his eyes.

"Thank you, sweetie." He pulled me to him for another hug. "I appreciate all you've done." His voice was quiet and husky with emotion. I knew he meant it. I just wished he'd been able to express it during my visit, rather than as I was leaving. We had so little time together — it was heartbreaking that so much of it was spent in tense anticipation of what was around the next sentence. He leaned back. "Now get going. And don't worry about us. We'll be fine."

In the car I turned back and waved. He was standing in the door, watching as we pulled out of the driveway.

Chapter 19

September slid into October and the leaves on the trees started their colorful death march. Green to red to brown to . . . gone. By Halloween, bare branches reached towards a cold, dark sky.

After my hurricane visit, I'd started calling my father and Helen every evening. Those calls haunted my days and nights like ghosts floating along the sidewalks on All Hallows Eve.

Wilson had hired a wonderfully competent woman who was with them every day. Wilson, Cindy, Bettie, and David stopped by often and did as much as they could, but unfortunately, Dad and Helen still had to manage evenings and large blocks of weekend time on their own. As Helen's health deteriorated, so did my father's disposition. When I called, I often heard him yelling in the background, in the middle of a tirade about something.

"Don't worry honey, I can handle him," she would assure me. Telling me not to worry was like telling a person afraid of heights not to feel ill while standing at the edge of the Grand Canyon. All I did was worry.

I flew back down for a long weekend in October and had reservations to go back the weekend before Thanksgiving. My visits didn't accomplish much, but they made me feel like I was doing something. Besides, he was my father, and I felt a responsibility to take some of the burden off those who were there every day.

Paul was pretty much gone Monday through Friday. The day-to-day responsibility for the boys' play dates, homework, and lives in general, as well as the daily maintenance of a 200-year-old farmhouse and — oh yeah — running my growing little business, all landed squarely on my shoulders.

Amidst all this, Santiago and I finally had all the paperwork ready for Trader Joe's.

"Lindsay, what do you think about coming out here for the meeting with the buyer?" he asked one afternoon.

"Do you think it's necessary?" *How am I going to do that? How can I afford it? When will I find the time?*

"It can't hurt. The owner of the company coming all the way from New Hampshire would certainly make a positive impression. Think about it. We don't need to make a decision now."

"I couldn't do it until after Thanksgiving." *Paul is gone and I have the kids and then I have to go to Virginia and we're hosting Thanksgiving here and . . . I think I'm drowning.*

"That's fine." Santiago was always so calm and measured. He seemed unflappable. I was envious. "This is nothing to stress out over. It was just an idea."

Stressed? Who me?

I checked my watch. Time to pick up the boys at school. After hanging up, I headed for the garage, but didn't get far. Suddenly, my heart was pounding so hard and erratically I felt like it was trying to jump out of my body. I could feel the vibration up into my throat. *Good God.* I lowered myself into the nearest chair. The pounding lasted for what seemed like an eternity, but was probably less than ten seconds. As suddenly as it began, it stopped. My heart settled back in my chest. I sat still a minute. All was quiet. I got up out of the chair and headed again for the garage.

Later, when the boys were getting ready for bed, I slowly finished kitchen clean-up. As soon as I was done, I would have to make my nightly call to the house on the Pagan River, and I dreaded those calls more than I could put into words. Bending over to put soap into the dishwasher, the pounding in my chest began again. I caught my breath, straightened up, and stood stock-still. *What the. . .* Just as before, the episode lasted mere seconds but seemed like an eternity. I took a couple of deep breaths and told myself it was nothing.

The next day, I called my doctor, but foolishly downplayed my fear and concern. They made an appointment for an echocardiogram and a twenty-four-hour heart monitor at the end of the week. Over the next couple of days the heart-pounding episodes increased in frequency and duration, but I refused to take myself to the hospital. Like most ex–Emergency Room nurses, I had a bizarre fear of going to the ER and being told nothing was wrong. My idiotic pride would simply not allow for that possibility.

The night before the appointment, I settled both boys in bed and kissed them goodnight. Paul was away, and I was looking forward to a quiet hour in front of some mindless television. I'd just started down the stairs when a bout of erratic pounding hit. It seemed to go on forever. I was terrified it wasn't going to stop. As I huddled on the stairs, I lowered my head onto my knees and began to pray. *Please God, don't let me die. I am so scared. Please don't let me die. My boys need me to be here. They need me. I am so scared. Please don't let me die.* I sat there for a long time — long after the pounding had stopped, and my heart rate returned to normal. I kept whispering to God, hoping to make him understand that I had to be here, that there were people who needed me. It would be six years before I would know for sure that my fervent prayers had been heard.

The cardiologist leaned forward in his chair and studied me. "Mrs. Frucci," he asked quietly, "is there anything going on in your life that's causing stress?"

Where do I start? I gave him a very brief snapshot of my life.

He smiled sympathetically. "You have enough on your plate to stress several people."

I managed a quivering smile and fought back tears. *I am just so fucking tired.*

His face softened. "What you're experiencing," he continued, "is atrial fibrillation, more commonly known as heart palpitations. They're often brought on by stress and can become self-perpetuating. What I mean is, they start because you're stressed, and then you worry about them and they get worse and you worry more and they get even worse. Does that make sense?"

I nodded silently. I'd played the strong, competent wife/mother/daughter/business-owner role so convincingly, for so long, that even I'd believed it. I was staggered by the fact that my body — especially my heart — had reacted in such a way. The "I-can-handle-anything-I-have-broad-shoulders" persona that I'd been holding onto with a vise-like grip was swept away without warning, and into the void whooshed a fatigue so overwhelming that all I wanted to do was put my head on this stranger's shoulder and cry until there were no more tears.

"You need to find a way to alleviate some of the stress."

And you would suggest I do that how??

"At the very least, I'd like you to practice some deep-breathing exercises at night before you go to sleep. They'll help you sleep more soundly and wake more rested." He handed me a sheet of paper with instructions and diagrams on it. "And Mrs. Frucci? Your heart is completely normal."

I took a deep, shaky breath and thanked him. He shook my hand and exited the examining room. I sat for a minute collecting myself, then wearily stood and hoisted my "I-can-handle-anything" persona back into place. It settled over me like a heavy coat and I could feel its weight pulling me back to reality. Straightening my shoulders, I walked out through the waiting room and into the chill of an early November afternoon.

Chapter 20

The afternoon sun of a warm December Friday washed over me, making the kitchen a cozy oasis. Sitting at my table/desk, I gazed through the sliding doors. Across the dirt road, the apple trees' gnarled branches cast their shadows against the red barn; in the distance, the fire tower atop Mount Kearsarge was visible against the clear blue sky. Stretched out on the warm bricks of the patio, both dogs were enjoying this gift of unseasonable warmth. Oscar, our enormous black cat, sat on the granite step keeping watch over his canine siblings.

To the casual observer it would appear I was drawing peace from the pastoral tableau outside my door. The casual observer would be wrong. I had a phone pressed against my ear and Santiago and I were finalizing plans for our meeting with Trader Joe's.

I'd be gone for thirty-six hours, which included fourteen hours of travel time — all for a thirty-minute meeting. And I was excited! At that moment it sounded "jet-setty," adventurous, and somehow very grown-up.

I squinted as I worked to dig something out of my overstuffed brain. *Damn, what was it?* "Oh, I know what I wanted to ask you." *Critically important question.* "What's the dress code?"

"It's a very casual culture," Santiago replied. "But I always wear a suit. I feel it sets the right tone of respect."

"That's what I needed to know." *Don't own a suit, can't afford one.*

"I'll pick you up at your hotel at eight," he continued. "I've got samples of the mix and all the paperwork, so you just need to bring yourself. Did you get an appointment with Karen?"

There were only three Trader Joe's stores on the East Coast so far, but Santiago had heard that their plans for expansion were aggressive. Karen was the East Coast buyer. Even if we could convince the West Coast to give the mixes a try, that didn't mean the East Coast would. But as soon as I'd told her I had a meeting out West, she'd agreed to see me.

"I have a really good feeling about this," Santiago said when I told him.

Paul was far less enthusiastic than Santiago. Especially since I'd walked away from my real-estate "career" completely.

"It's a long way to go for one thirty-minute meeting."

I know.

"Do you realize how much this is gonna cost?"

I do.

"Can't this broker guy handle it? Isn't that why you hired him?"

Probably and yes.

So why was I going? Because my "gut" told me it was the right thing to do, and because I trusted the opinion of this man I had met only once.

At Trader Joe's East Coast headquarters, Karen's warm, friendly handshake put me immediately at ease. Once we settled in her cubby, I opened the brownies and slid them across the desk towards her. She chose one, took a cautious bite and an "Oh-my-God-I-didn't-expect-this!" expression lit up her face.

She waved the partially eaten brownie in the air. "People have to try these to understand how good they are." She popped the piece in her mouth. "Your mix and our yogurt would make a perfect demo." She absently licked the remaining crumbs off her thumb and forefinger before reaching for a napkin.

She's gonna approve it!

"I love them. I'll present them to the committee at our meeting on Friday."

Committee? Apparently, all new products were taste-tested and approved by committee. She took her recommendations to them, but it was a team decision. In fact, she would have to take a package of mix home and bake it herself for the taste testing.

The brownies were good enough on their own to convince most people, but some people thought anything fat-free was taste-free. When it came to my brownies,

I was the best person to persuade people to overcome that mind-set but this time it was out of my hands.

Karen assured me she'd call Friday, after the meeting. I thanked her, climbed into the Explorer and headed to Logan Airport.

I was three hours early for my flight to L.A. At a pay phone in a quiet corner, I made my daily call to Virginia.

Helen was following No Pudge! with great interest and wanted all the details of my day. After listening on the extension for a while, Dad politely said he needed to get back to his paints and hung up. It was one of the better calls we'd had in a long time. I wished I could get away with calling in the afternoon every day.

Ten hours later I landed at LAX, bone-tired and travel-grubby. I couldn't wait to hit a hot shower and a soft bed.

"That will be room 1548. Do you need help with your bag?"

"No, thank you." *I have one small bag. Do I look incapable of handling it?*

"The elevators are across the lobby on the right. Enjoy your stay, Mrs. Frucci."

It was only ten p.m. California time, but according to my body and brain it was one o'clock in the morning.

I got off the elevator on the fifteenth floor and followed the signs toward my room. I came to the end of one long corridor, only to turn left onto another.

Could my room be any farther from the elevator? My one small suitcase was getting heavier by the minute. *C'mon already.* The corridor dead-ended at a set of double doors with the number "1548" on them. I rechecked the number on my key card. 1548. *Okay*. . . I slid the card into the slot, turned the handle, and walked in. Even in the dark I could tell this wasn't a standard room. As the door closed quietly behind me, I flipped on the light switch. The soft glow of table lamps illuminated a lavishly decorated living room. Laughing, I explored the large suite. Living room, dining room, kitchenette, and two large bedrooms, each with its own huge bathroom. In both bathrooms, snow-white towels, so thick they barely fit over the towel bars, hung above enormous soaking tubs and gleaming gray marble vanities.

Paul had made my reservation, and the combination of his status as a Hilton "frequent sleeper" and my late arrival had gotten me an upgrade to the lap of luxury. I was going to be there — alone — for less than ten hours.

I chose a bedroom and put my suitcase on the upholstered bench at the end of the king-size bed. Pulling out a pair of slacks, I opened the closet door. Inside were two white robes. Reaching out, I slid my hand over the silky fabric. *I could get used to this.* I pulled one off the hanger, grabbed my toothbrush, and sashayed into my opulent marble bath.

At 7:45 the next morning, dressed in gray wool pants, a white blouse, and black blazer — my sparse closet's nod to a suit — I reluctantly exited my luxurious home-for-a-night and made the long walk to the elevators, pulling my suitcase behind me. On a seat outside the main door, I settled down to wait for Santiago in the crisp chill of an early-winter Southern California morning.

A large black American sedan pulled up and a gentleman dressed in a wool topcoat and black leather gloves stepped out. With a smile, he headed in my direction. "You made it!" We hugged like old friends. "How was your trip?" Before I could answer, he added, "Aren't you cold?"

"It's not cold," I laughed. "You're dressed like it's winter!"

He grinned. "This is freezing for us." He grabbed the handle of my suitcase and walked me to his car. During breakfast and the short ride to Trader Joe's headquarters we chatted comfortably. When we walked in the door, the receptionist greeted Santiago warmly.

"Amy's waiting for you."

As we wound our way through the maze of low-walled cubbies, Santiago greeted everyone by name. It was clear he felt comfortable here.

At the end of an aisle, a petite, thirty-something Asian woman stood waiting for us, her posture as straight as the black hair that fell smoothly to her jaw. Santiago introduced me and we settled ourselves in her cubbie, where he placed the brownies he had made onto her desk.

She shook her head. Her sleek hair slid towards her face, and she quickly tucked it behind her ears. "No, thank you."

Whad'ya mean? I came all the way out here and you aren't even going to try them?!

"I'm not a big chocolate person." She smiled to soften the blow. "But I'll put them out by the coffee. I'm sure they'll be devoured and I'll get lots of feedback."

Not great, but okay.

Santiago and I took turns talking about the brownies and the consumer reaction. She sat quietly, her dark eyes intent, an occasional slight nodding of her head the only movement. When it was clear we were done lauding the wonder of "Brownies without Guilt," she turned to me.

"Lindsay, I want you to know how impressed I am you came all the way out here for this meeting."

Good start.

She leaned on the desk and folded long, slim fingers. "But I also have to tell you, I have serious reservations about your mix making it in the California market."

My heart plummeted into my stomach like a boulder pushed off a cliff. *What?*

"Californians — especially Southern Californians — don't bake," she continued. "If they want brownies, they buy them already made. And every product we carry must achieve strict weekly sales levels. To be honest, I don't see No Pudge! being able to hit and maintain those levels."

But I came all this way. . . .

Santiago said something to her about how unique they were, but it barely registered.

She addressed me again. "If I were willing to give them a try, would you consider doing private label?"

Lesson #3 in Grocery Industry 101: Amy was suggesting she might carry No Pudge! if I agreed to pack the mix in a Trader Joe's bag. No pink label, no smiling pig, no No Pudge!. Private label is a no-brainer for big manufacturers who already have a solid brand, but a tough call for a small company struggling to establish one.

My response was purely instinctual. "The brand is all I have." I leaned towards her. I was speaking from my soul. "No Pudge! is tiny. Any big company could come up with a similar product tomorrow and put me out of business. Establishing this brand as quickly as possible is the only thing protecting me. I can't just give it away." I sat back and looked at her. "I can't."

The only sound in the small cubbie was the low hum from the activity outside its walls. Amy leaned back in her chair, her eyes still on my face, her only movement a slow twisting of the simple gold band on her left hand. I could almost see the wheels turning in her mind. "Let me give this some thought," she finally said as she sat forward and picked up her pen. "But I will tell you two things: first, your pricing is too high for us." She looked at Santiago.

"We might be able to make some adjustments." He looked at me and I nodded. I had no idea how we'd find more room in the price, but he seemed confident, so I kept my mouth shut.

"Good. Second," she looked at me, "if I were to make a recommendation to the committee that we bring this in, it would be with the stipulation we drop it in the spring. Baking mixes don't sell in the summer. If the sales numbers are strong enough, I would consider bringing it back in the fall, but I'm not promising anything." She paused and her fingers once again strayed to the gold band. The wheels were turning and it wasn't helping my cause any. "I honestly don't see a fat-free mix selling well during the holidays," she continued, "so I probably wouldn't consider bringing it back until the first of next year. At best, I see this as a winter-only product."

Two days, two appointments, and two very definite "maybes."

"I just hope you'll give it a chance."

"I will certainly give it serious thought." She stood. "Once again, I want you to know how much I appreciate your coming all this way." She held out her hand. "I will be in touch with Santiago in the next couple of days." Our meeting was over.

As soon as we got through the door, Santiago gave my arm a gentle squeeze. "I know that wasn't what we were hoping for, but she didn't say no. She was very impressed by your coming here and may give it a chance based on that."

"But what about pricing?" We walked across the tree-shaded parking lot. "I gave it my best shot."

"Let's see what she's looking for. I'll give her a day to think about it and call her tomorrow afternoon." He stopped at the car and took off his coat. "Warming up." He folded it carefully. "Guess I don't need this anymore."

"You didn't need it in the first place!" I teased.

Pulling up in front of the American Airlines terminal, Santiago handed my suitcase to the check-in valet before turning to me. "Don't be discouraged," he said. "I still think we have a good shot."

I trudged to my gate, dreading the call I would have to make. Not to my father and Helen, but to Paul. I steeled myself for the "I told you so" and dialed. He got a big kick out of the story about my elaborate accommodations the night before. But when I told him how the appointments had gone, to his credit and my surprise, the dreaded the four words didn't pass his lips. He simply said he was sorry the trip hadn't worked out the way I'd hoped. The "I told you so" was all mine.

"I have good news and bad news," Santiago said when he called Thursday afternoon.

Amy had agreed to place one trial order — if, and it was a big if, we could get the price a lot lower. She'd suggested a target retail price that was so low, I immediately told him there was no way.

In a no-nonsense, we're-not-giving-up-that-easily tone, he said, "I know this seems impossible, but let's think about it."

I sat down at my table/desk with paper and calculator.

"Maybe your co-packer would give you a better rate on big runs of just Original," Santiago said. "How about we make the minimum order ten thousand pounds? Are you doing runs that big now?"

"Ten thousand pounds? Are you kidding me? I've just gotten up to a thousand."

By the time we were done I had a list of questions for Peter, and the glimmer of hope that maybe, just maybe, we could make this work.

"See," he said. "We just needed to get creative."

"Without you, I wouldn't have had a clue how to get this kind of creative. Thanks for not giving up on me."

"Give up on you? I'd never do that."

After I hung up, the realization hit me that No Pudge! wasn't just a vague, someday fantasy anymore. It was real. My baby was growing before my eyes. And I had a team of people who offered guidance, wisdom, and, best of all, support. "Give up on you?" Santiago had sounded surprised I would even suggest such a thing. I had a feeling the others would feel the same way.

Paul's office door opened. He walked down the hall and into the kitchen, the ever-present coffee mug in hand. "Isn't it time to pick up the boys?" he asked as he headed for the coffee pot. "And what are we doing about dinner?"

I can always count on you to bring me back to reality. "I'm leaving now and I'll pick something up when I'm in town. Any requests?" From business owner to mother/wife/homemaker faster than you can say "No Pudge!"

Ob-La-Di, Ob-La-Da, life goes o-on. La-la-la-la life goes on.

Chapter 21

"The tasting went very well." True to her word, Karen had called as soon as the new-product committee meeting was over.

How come she doesn't sound very upbeat?

"But," she continued. "We've decided to stick with our full-fat brownie mix for now. I'm sorry. I tried."

"That's okay." I slumped back in my chair. "It's not your fault." The weight of disappointment was so intense that I could feel my body getting heavier.

"How did your appointment in Pasadena go?" she asked.

Huh? I was having trouble moving past the part where they'd decided to stick to the full-fat mix. I struggled to an upright position, explained about the proposal for Amy, and told her I thought our chances were pretty good. I left out the part about it being a seasonal product.

"I'll keep an eye on sales if you get in there. If it does well, I'll have a much stronger case. No matter what, feel free to stay in touch with me." She was trying to make me feel better. My gloom must have been flowing right through the telephone line.

After hanging up, I immediately collapsed back into a slump. *Whatif all this work is for nothing? Whatif the brownies really aren't that good? Whatif I really can't grow this business big enough to make money?* My friends the whatifs were pushing their way in with a vengeance. I sat up straight. *Shake this off, girl. Move on. You can do this.* I picked up my pen and made a note to call Karen again in a couple of months. A plan. I felt better already.

A couple of days before Christmas, Santiago called with the best present I got that year. Amy had decided to give No Pudge! a try and would be placing an order right after the first of the year. She warned him it was a trial. If they didn't sell well, she wouldn't order again. I hardly heard him. I'd gotten into Trader Joe's West! A hundred stores! That number alone seemed staggering.

The boost stayed with me through the holidays. Then one night in early January, it culminated in what became one of the highlights of my No Pudge! journey. I was snuggling with the boys in front of the TV, when Paul walked in with a dazed expression on his face.

"This just came through on the fax." He handed me a piece of paper. It was a purchase order from Trader Joe's West for 480 24-pack cases of No Pudge! Original Fudge Brownie Mix. 11,520 bags. $27,563.70. For No

Pudge!. They wanted $27,563.70-worth of *my* brownie mix.

Eyes wide, I looked up at Paul.

He was beaming. "Didn't you expect this? Didn't you know how much it would be for?"

I shook my head slightly to clear it. "I-I was so caught up with the per-case price, I never added it up." I looked down at it again. *Yup, still says $27,563.70.*

By now the kids were clamoring to see the paper. They hooted and hollered and offered high-fives.

"Way to go, Mom."

"That's awesome! Congratulations, Mom!"

"Yeah, honey, congratulations. This *is* awesome." Paul pulled me up and gave me a big hug.

That night, Paul took his first step towards becoming a No Pudge! "believer." It was also the night he took the first wobbly steps in his journey of getting to really know the woman he'd been married to for sixteen years. This woman was, in fact, a new acquaintance for both of us, but I pretended I'd known she was there all along.

Chapter 22

My sister's oldest son and I sat at the ancient kitchen table in the house on the Pagan River, lingering over a second cup of coffee. Still in pj's and bed-head, we were travel-weary and bleary-eyed.

"When's the limo supposed to be here?" Erik asked.

I glanced at the clock. "About an hour and a half. We should probably make sure he's set, and then get ourselves ready."

Our beloved "Grammy Helen" had quietly slipped away two days earlier. Today was her funeral. I knew Helen would have agreed with my decision not to have Paul and the boys make the trip, but I'd dreaded spending these few days alone with my dad. I was relieved when my twenty-eight-year-old nephew said he was coming. Erik had the luxury of being one generation removed, and I knew that, in order to maintain his reputation as the endearingly eccentric grandfather, my father would work hard to be on his best behavior. The complex history my father and I shared, and my frustration at being treated like a not-very-bright child, got in the way of my ability to be patient.

I rose to my feet and stretched. "All right. I'm movin'."

Erik yawned loudly and dropped his head on his arms. "I'm going back to sleep."

"Get up, you!" I tossed a dish towel at the back of his blond head. "I'm not doing this alone."

"I need some help down here!" The call of an annoyed old man found its way to the kitchen.

"There's the happy camper now." I grinned at Erik. "You're a guy — you should help him get dressed."

"Me?" He grimaced. "You're his daughter. That's your privilege." He cocked his head. "Auntie Lin, did I just hear a car pull in?"

"Good God, I certainly hope not."

We hurried to the foyer and peeked through the sidelights.

A strange car was parked in the driveway. As we watched two more cars pulled in behind it.

Erik and I looked at each other for a horrified second. In case you haven't fully gotten it: I am in my pajamas and my hair is sticking straight out from my head. Erik hasn't shaved and is wearing a wife-beater undershirt and shorts. We're both barefoot. My father is in his bedroom in some state of undress. We are Northern outsiders in a small, proper Southern town, and it appears we are about to be the unwitting hosts of a pre-funeral get-together.

The car doors opened and people dressed in sedate, funereal attire began to climb out. Not a familiar face among them. Like clown cars at a circus, people kept coming out.

Frozen, we stood and stared.

Then from down the hall came a pissed-off growl. "Goddamn it, isn't anybody listening to me? I am standing here stark naked and need some help!" That sentence and the visual it prompted were enough to jolt us out of our trance.

Without a word, I started towards the kitchen, Erik right on my heels. When I came to a screeching where-am-I-going-what-am-I-doing halt, he crashed into me. Taking a quick step back, he turned back towards the door and I started towards the bedroom. We stopped simultaneously and looked at each other. The expression on his face reminded me of when a friend popped a chip with a big glob of what she thought was guacamole into her mouth. It was wasabi.

I started laughing uncontrollably. "Oh my God, Erik."

He looked at me like I was deranged. "Are you all right?"

Gasping, I shook my head and wiped my eyes. "Who the hell are these people?" We could hear voices as the crowd made their way across the driveway towards the front door. *Get it together, kid. Fast.* "Okay," I said. "Here's what we're gonna do."

Erik poised like a sprinter waiting for the starting gun.

"You go get some clothes on him. I'll deal with them."

"Greeaat." Erik moaned. "Bumpa naked. Can't wait."

"Wanna trade?" I asked sweetly.

"Coming, Bumpa," Erik called as he headed down the hall.

I raked my fingers through the mop on my head, put my hand on the knob, and looked heavenward where I was absolutely sure Helen was happily settled, getting a big kick out of this whole scenario. "Couldn't you have warned me?!" Then, fixing what I hoped was a warm, welcoming smile on my face, I opened the door.

Helen's family from Northern Virginia was almost as stunned to see a strange woman in her pajamas open the door as I had been to see them pull in the driveway. They apologized profusely, offering to turn around and head directly into town, but I insisted they make themselves comfortable in the living room. I put on another pot of coffee and excused myself. My father was just about dressed, so I closed my bedroom door and quickly dialed Wilson.

"You'd better get over here — and fast," I hissed into the phone when he answered. "We have company."

Helen had lived in Smithfield her entire adult life, and it seemed everyone over the age of sixty had come to the large church to say their goodbyes. Sitting in the front pew with my arm tight against my father's, listening to the minister, a sharp feeling of *déjà vu* engulfed me. It had been twenty-five years since my mother had died. I tried to tell myself I was blessed to have had two such amazing women in my life, but losing both felt so unfair. *Yeah, I know. Life isn't fair.* But if they'd joined forces now, I was in luck. Those two would make a team of guardian angels the fates would not want to mess with. Somehow Mom and Helen together seemed right. Sending a prayer heavenward to whoever was listening, I silently pleaded, *Please let me be around for my boys for a very long time.*

I stole a glance at my father. He held his head high and his eyes were dry, but he looked small and old. I slipped my hand into his and he gave it a squeeze.

After the service we stood in the vestibule thanking people for coming. My father was gracious and charming, ready with warm handshakes, cheek kisses, and promises to accept dinner invitations that would probably never come as people went back to their busy lives. The issue of where he was going to live now that Helen was gone loomed large in my mind. He wouldn't be gracious and charming when that conversation took place.

The next morning, Erik headed into town for the paper. My father settled into his favorite chair with a book. I stood in the hall outside the living room, trying to get up the courage to face the tempest I knew was coming. I lifted my chin. *Here goes. . .* "Dad, we need to talk."

I told him how Wilson and I had carefully reviewed all the options. I explained that Wilson, Bettie, and David had been to see the assisted living facility in town, that it was warm and homey and, because it was new, had rooms available. By staying in Smithfield, he would still be surrounded by all his friends and I would continue to visit regularly. As I expected, what we thought didn't matter.

"I am perfectly capable of staying here on my own." He was angry and insistent.

"I don't blame you for wanting to stay here, but will you just go with me and look?" I knew I was pleading with a brick wall, still I pushed on. "Please try to be open-minded. I think you'll be surprised." I had remained standing, hoping my height would discourage his demoting me to child status. It didn't work.

His voice rose in sharp-edged anger, a tone I knew all too well. "Now, you listen to me, little girl. I am staying here and that's final. This conversation is over." When he started throwing "little girl" at me, I knew there was no point pushing further unless I wanted this to escalate into something ugly — which I desperately did not.

I walked to the bedroom, closed the door, and sat heavily on the bed. Now what? I called Wilson, who agreed this was a battle not yet worth fighting. We'd let him stay in the house for a couple of months and monitor him closely. My father had never been independent or solitary. We hoped he'd realize being alone was not what he wanted.

Dad was happy with our decision. Why not? He'd won.

Back home, it was turning into a warmer than normal winter. In northern New England, that didn't translate into balmy breezes and early daffodils, but rather freezing rain that turned roads into black-ice skating rinks. It sucked.

Luckily, there was a bright spot. And its name was Trader Joe's. Amy wasn't reporting killer sales, but they were steady enough that she was happy. Plus, Trader Joe's was driving the mail-order business. People kept telling me they'd heard about the mix because their sister/mother/best friend had bought it at Trader Joe's and told them about it.

Although I was ecstatic, I was spending huge chunks of time chatting with customers and writing orders. Those conversations were the life-sustaining oxygen that kept me moving forward, but if No Pudge! was going to grow, I needed to spend my time talking to the store owners and buyers who could reach whole cities of customers.

The World Wide Web was in its fledgling state, but people were starting to ask about ordering online. No Pudge! needed its own website. Bob and Jay thought I also needed one more No Pudge! flavor to round out the line.

My High Priority To-Do List was rearing its ugly, top-heavy head. "Get Into More Stores" entrenched itself into the highest slot, constantly daring me to knock it off. My constant companion, it was the overlying theme and mantra of the next eight years.

The items just below that one changed constantly. For the winter of 1997 they were: find a reputable web designer and work with her to design the perfect customer-friendly website with ordering capabilities, *and* create the formula for a fourth flavor, get it into production and onto store shelves. No big deal really. Oh yeah — and run the house, manage the family, call my dad, fly to Virginia, and Get Into More Stores. Piece of cake. Or brownie. . .

By the time the sleety, freezing rain warmed enough to melt the dirty piles of snow along the roadways, I'd gone back to my lab (a.k.a. my kitchen) and come up with a formula for a Mint Fudge brownie that my skiing buddies declared a winner. The website was making slow but steady progress. Get Into More Stores still taunted me from atop its secure perch, but Karen had come through with an order for Trader Joe's East, so for the moment it was satiated.

Chapter 23

Early April in northern New England is bleak. The landscape is still brown, and heavy gray clouds unleash cold rain. I was sitting in the kitchen, watching the rain fall and trying to find comfort in a steaming mug of tea, when Santiago called.

With orders coming every few weeks all winter, we'd assured ourselves that Amy would reconsider letting inventory run out in the spring. Not only had she not reconsidered, she wouldn't even commit to bringing the mix back in the fall. "Maybe in January" was the best Santiago could get.

The good news was, Karen from Trader Joe's East had no plans to stop ordering. Unfortunately, she ordered for four stores. Amy ordered for over a hundred.

The bleakness of April continued when Paul and I headed to Virginia to move my dad into assisted living.

Over the winter it had become clear it wasn't safe for him to live alone. Wilson and I had decided the time had come. I didn't want to tell him we'd already made a decision since his reaction to any "done deal" announcement would be vicious. I thought if he had a chance to see the assisted living home for himself, he'd realize living there wasn't such a bad idea.

I knew his refusal to tour the place was more pride and pigheadedness than desire to continue living alone. So when I was visiting in March, I firmly informed him — in the no-nonsense voice I usually reserved for my children — that he had a choice. He could visit willingly with an open mind or he could kick and scream all the way there. Either way, he was going. Period.

"I'll look, but I can tell you right now, little girl, I am not moving there."

Rather than argue, I simply thanked him and then warned the director that dear old Dad was adamantly opposed to a move.

We slowly made our way from the bright foyer with its fresh flowers through a living room, tastefully furnished with comfortable chairs and sofas. Looking up from where they were working on a large puzzle, two diminutive, gray-haired ladies smiled and nodded. The director laid her hand gently on my father's arm and told him how honored they would be to have an artist of such distinction living there. Would he consider giving a class? Yes, it was completely understandable he wasn't interested in teaching anymore. A demonstration maybe? He would? How wonderful!

We moved slowly into the dining room, where upholstered dining chairs were tucked neatly under tables set with white linens.

"We serve three meals a day here," she explained, and should there be any food that he particularly craved, why all he had to do was ask. They had a big, light-filled room that she thought would be perfect for him. Would he like to have a look?

By the time I got him back in the car he was admitting that moving there might not be so bad. Before he could say "assisted living," I'd signed the papers and arranged to move him at the end of April.

Paul and I left for Virginia on the last Thursday in April and drove straight through. With the help of Bettie, David, Wilson, and Cindy, we spent Friday, Saturday, and Sunday getting him organized, moved, and settled. He insisted on packing his own paints, brushes, and canvasses. All were painstakingly wrapped, labeled, and placed carefully in boxes. Helen had lived in the house for forty years before my father came on the scene, and he'd arrived with little more than his clothes and art supplies. He wasn't leaving with much more. A bed, dresser, his favorite chair, the television, and his easel were loaded in the U-Haul with his clothes and art supplies.

"I think that's everything." Trying to remove the sweat and grime that had built up over the long day, I wiped my face and neck with a couple of paper towels soaked with cold water.

Dad was leaning on his walker by the door. He'd unbuttoned his shirt and beneath the sparse gray hair, his thin chest was shiny with sweat.

"Ready to go?" I asked. "We should get moving if we want to get everything unloaded before dark."

He nodded. "I'm ready."

Closing the old porch door for the last time, I held on to his arm as he made his way down the two cracked concrete steps. *He feels so frail.* As he maneuvered his walker across the driveway to the car, I walked close beside him, my hand resting on the small of his back. He was leaving the home he had known for twenty years, most probably making the last move of his life. When we reached the car, he turned and gazed back at the house one last time.

"It's been a good old house," he said quietly, almost to himself.

"Yes, Dad, it has. You and Helen had a wonderful life here." I lightly rubbed his shoulders. He stood for one more moment then sighed and carefully settled himself in the passenger seat. Paul got behind the wheel. I climbed in the back behind him. As we slowly pulled out of the driveway, I noticed that Dad determinedly stared straight ahead. He did not look back — not once.

Late Sunday, Paul and I got in the car and drove back to New Hampshire. We stopped only for the all-nighter necessities: fast-food burgers and fries, coffee, and then the inevitable too-many-cups-of-coffee pee breaks. Arriving home in the wee hours Monday morning, we crawled into bed. When the alarm rang at its usual work-/school-day early hour, I felt like my head had just hit the pillow. A full workweek loomed. As I struggled to open two bleary eyes, a bright thought found its way through the fog. *April's almost over!* Just a few more days until this damn month hit the history books. May had to be better. It was hard to imagine how it could be much worse.

Chapter 24

We stood side by side with our noses pressed against the hotel window, taking in the unobstructed view across the Chicago River to the city's spectacular, sparkling, late-night skyline.

We were four wiped-out country bumpkins in the Big City for the annual Food Marketing Institute (FMI) Show. The state of New Hampshire bought booth space every year to promote New Hampshire–based food companies and offered exhibit space for a nominal fee. I knew very little about the show other than it was supposed to be huge.

Wendy's company produced gourmet chocolates, Louise offered a dry mix for the scones she had grown up making in her native England, and Gail, a six-foot-tall, blonde farmer's daughter, was one of the senior people at the New Hampshire Department of Agriculture. She was responsible for the booth at the show.

The next morning we woke early to board the shuttle bus. In my opinion, Chicago in the spring should be on every traveler's "bucket list." Tall tulips in yellow and red waved at us from the planters lining Michigan Avenue. The park that runs the length of the city along Lake Michigan was alive with forsythia bushes and beds of hyacinth, daffodils, and ever more tulips. The magnificent fountains gushed water and the grass was already lush. We had left a still-sad, barely greening New Hampshire behind and landed in Oz. Twenty minutes later, the bus pulled up to a huge glass-and-steel complex on the shore of Lake Michigan and we joined the throngs pouring through the doors. Entering the vast exhibit hall, we took a moment to absorb the magnitude of the scene.

Companies like Nabisco, Coca-Cola, and Kraft introduce their newest offerings at FMI and spend unfathomable amounts on gargantuan booths, many with second stories and some with balconies and "roof-top" patios. The hall was lit by brilliant overheads that sharpened the already-bright colors of the booths. Like the Fancy Food Show, the atmosphere was carnivalesque, but on a grander scale.

As we wandered the aisles in search of our space, we passed the Philip Morris booth. The size of a small house, it included a smoking room where miniskirted cowgirls (the Marlboro Girl clearly being deemed more of a draw than the Marlboro Man) waited to pass out cigarettes to anyone who wanted them. Other booths were ready with slot machines or video games, and everywhere scantily clad, model-beautiful women were poised to pass out samples and be the eye candy that would draw people to the booth.

We found our postage-sized space nestled with the other small booths in the low-rent district far from the "midway." We helped Gail set out the New Hampshire products she'd brought and tried to arrange our samples on the few square inches left over.

At ten o'clock the aisles filled. We spent the next couple of hours handing out samples and chatting with prospective customers. I wrote a couple of small orders, but I was starting to realize these were the "big grocery" guys. And by guys, I mean only guys. "Anyone else notice there aren't any women here?" I asked during a break in the activity. "This is, like, 99 percent men in suits."

Wendy laughed. "Come on, there are women — the booths are full of 'em."

"Cowgirls in miniskirts don't count." The realization that this was such a male-dominated industry was unsettling. "Seriously, what's wrong with this picture?" Before we could get into a good, indignant, this-isn't-fair-but-watch-us-change-things discussion, the sound of brass instruments and drums suddenly vibrated through the hall.

Attendees about-faced and exhibitors started abandoning their booths to head in the direction of the music. As we neared the entrance, we watched in disbelief while an endless parade of high-school kids in blue-and-silver band uniforms poured in, marching with military precision. For the next half hour they high-stepped up one aisle and down the other, trombones and trumpets swinging and bass drums booming. It was totally bizarre.

The next two days weren't nearly as entertaining. We passed out countless samples of brownies, chocolates, and scones, but we were out of our league. There weren't many buyers looking for unique, small-company products.

Friends in the industry kept telling me to forget about the big grocery chains, saying it was too tough a playing field for a small company like mine. "Focus on getting the mixes into more natural-food stores," I was told over and over. But I believed No Pudge! belonged in big grocery stores. I had come to this show hoping to reach a big chain buyer. It wasn't happening.

By noon the last day, the number of attendees wandering through the low-rent district had dwindled.

"Think I'll take a walk around the midway and see what the 'other half' is up to. You guys cover for me?" We'd listened to each other's spiel nonstop for two and a half days. In the unlikely chance that someone important stopped by, any one of my comrades-in-arms could handle it. A chorus of "Go!" and "We've got it" followed me as I headed towards the high-rise booths looming in the distance.

I wandered past one elaborate booth after another with no destination in mind until I saw Ben & Jerry's. *Ice cream!* Heading towards the sampling table, I noticed a man who looked remarkably like my father in his younger days. Tall, slim, with graying hair and a trim mustache, he stood alone, quietly observing the ebb and flow of people lining up for cups of their favorite Ben & Jerry's flavor.

I abruptly halted my determined beeline to the booth and almost caused a pile-up. *Could this be the new CEO?!* As ice cream lovers detoured around me, I tried to read his badge without being too obvious. Perry something. It had to be him.

He's alone — I should go introduce myself.

Are you kidding me? He's the CEO of Ben & Jerry's!

So what? I'm the CEO of No Pudge!.

Yeah but. . .

C'mon, girl — you got nothin' to lose.

What the hell. . .

I took a deep breath, and walked up to him, trying to read his last name as quickly as possible. *Odak. That's sounds right.*

"Excuse me — Mr. Odak?"

He turned to me with a smile. "Yes?"

I held out my hand. "Lindsay Frucci."

"How do you do?"

So far so good.

"I own a company, No Pudge! Foods, and we manufacture all-natural, fat-free fudge brownie mixes." *We?* "The consumer just adds yogurt to the mix."

"Really?" He appeared genuinely interested.

I plowed on. "We're located in New Hampshire and I thought there might be a possibility of doing something together. Frozen yogurt with a fat-free brownie mix-in, for example? Still decadent but healthier." I stopped. I didn't know if his smile was one of interest or if he was simply amused that this woman from some company he'd never heard of had the chutzpah to approach him.

"Interesting. That sounds like something worth thinking about." He slipped a well-manicured hand into the pocket of his suit coat. "Do you have a card?"

"I do." I reached into the pocket of my apron.

"Why don't you send me information about your company and your product after the show?" He offered me his card. "I'll pass it along to my research and development team."

You will?! "Thank you so much!"

The babble of voices around me melted into an inconsequential hum as he held out his hand. "It was very nice meeting you."

"Nice meeting you, too." I gave him a firm businesslike shake and then walked away, grinning as though I'd just won the lottery. This could be huge.

As I floated back to the booth, visions of Ben & Jerry's newest sensation — No Pudge! Fudge Brownie Frozen Yogurt — danced in my head. Up until now I hadn't deemed the show a success, but one ninety-second conversation had changed all that.

On the flight home I allowed my mind to wander through all sorts of wonderful whatif scenarios.

The next day I sent Mr. Odak my company literature and samples. Back to the nonstop routine of work, house, kids, hubby, and pets, I relegated the Ben & Jerry's whatifs to the on-hold file in the back of my mind.

A week later on a mid-May afternoon, I was working my way through the daily people-to-call-and-leave-messages-for-'cause-no-one-answers-their-phone list, when my phone rang.

I sat in stunned silence while the voice introduced herself as the head of research and development at Ben & Jerry's. Perry Odak had asked her to set up a meeting. Would I be willing to come up to Burlington, Vermont, to meet with her?

The entire call lasted less than five minutes, but when it was over I had arranged what I hoped would be a life-changing meeting with the head of R & D for Ben & Jerry's Ice Cream.

The whatifs came roaring back. I sat there, my mind in happy fantasy overload and let them snowball on and on and on.

Chapter 25

In northern New England, May holds tantalizing promise. I was hoping that along with the daffodils and robins, the delicate May breeze would bring a sweet deal with Ben & Jerry's.

On the day of the Big Meeting, as I crossed the bridge over the Connecticut River that links New Hampshire to Vermont, that sweet deal, with all its implications, filled my head. As angular, tree-covered hills gave way to picture-postcard rolling green meadows, I envisioned happy ice cream pints dancing on piles of green dollars. I drove north on Interstate 89 to Burlington, where Ben and Jerry had opened their first scoop shop in an old gas station. When their ice cream became a national obsession, they'd established their headquarters and manufacturing facility there.

I cruised past family farms nestled in valleys between hills that looked like fat, green pillows. Spotted cows grazed contentedly beside large red barns with silver silos. The morning sun shone through the window, filling the car with warmth. I kept the radio off and enjoyed the quiet.

I felt good about today's meeting. After all, she had called me. I'd given a lot of thought to what I should take, and decided baked samples and a case of mix for her to "play with" in her test kitchen would do the trick. By the end of the meeting, I hoped we'd have some ideas for creative ways to work together.

Following her directions, I pulled off the highway at the appointed exit and did a bunch of right, left, right, left turns until I recognized what she had described as a "flat, ugly, brown building." After finding a parking place, I slung the long straps of the cooler and my briefcase over my shoulder, grabbed the case of mix and headed for the front door.

The lobby was nondescript except for the kind of ice cream pushcart you'd see on a summer street corner, with the familiar Ben & Jerry's graphics all over it. A hand-lettered sign encouraged visitors to PLEASE HELP YOURSELF.

On the way out for sure!

I spoke to the receptionist and very quickly a woman came out. Her face was framed with disheveled brown waves and she was dressed casually in khakis and a colorful cotton shirt. Smiling, she introduced herself as Mary, the woman I'd spoken to on the phone.

Glancing quickly at the cardboard box and cooler, she asked if I would need a computer or audio-visual equipment.

For what?

We walked down bright blue, yellow, and green hallways painted with life-sized replicas of the happy cow logo. It looked more like the inside of a daycare center than the headquarters of a multimillion-dollar corporation. The conference rooms we passed were named after their famous ice cream pints.

"Where's that meeting being held?" I could imagine one worker saying to another.

"Chunky Monkey. Two o'clock. See you there!"

As we turned a corner, Mary pointed out a large test kitchen on the left. My attention was on the kitchen, so it took me a second to realize that she had stopped at the open door of a large conference room. When I looked in, twenty pairs of eyes looked back expectantly. *Holy shit — what is this?* Word had gotten out that the new CEO had asked me to come and the troops were lined up to hear what I had to say.

The following thirty minutes of Embarrassment Hell are still an agonizing blur. The people in that room were plainly expecting a corporate-level presentation that would introduce them to my company and convince them to use No Pudge! in some new and innovative way. This was a corporation that had just reported sales of $167 million and here I was with a couple of pans of brownies.

It was like one of those dreams where you find yourself in a crowd of staring strangers and look down to discover the only thing you're wearing is your socks. But this wasn't a dream. I was fully dressed, yet felt completely exposed. My stomach was doing cartwheels, and although throwing up would have gotten me out of there, it would also have eliminated my last shred of dignity. I did my best to ad lib, but it took the folks in that conference room about ten seconds to figure out I was in so far over my head I couldn't see daylight. They were gracious and I tried to appear professional, but it was awkward and uncomfortable.

The meeting dragged on for close to thirty minutes. They politely explained that the yogurt in my brownies wouldn't freeze solid enough to work with their equipment. They also explained that the company currently making their brownies was a nonprofit organization whose employees were developmentally disabled. I had no response to either issue and could offer no alternatives. All I wanted was to get out of there.

Mary, who'd been sitting to my left throughout this ordeal, finally took pity on me and stood to signal that the meeting was over. People smiled, shook my hand, and thanked me for coming. I'm sure I responded appropriately, but I couldn't wait to escape to the sanctuary of my car. Back in the lobby, just the thought of ice cream added to my nausea. I had to work to keep my head up and my eyes dry as I walked across the parking lot. Once in the safety of the closed car, I leaned my forehead against the steering wheel and allowed the hot tears to roll down my cheeks.

"OhmyGodohmyGodohmyGod. I am *such* an idiot." My nose was now running along with the tears. Sniffling loudly and swearing like a frat boy, I rummaged unsuccessfully through my briefcase for something to stem the tide that was flowing all over my face. "Goddamn it." I took a deep, shaky breath and sat up straight, resorting to the back of my hand to wipe my nose and the heels of each palm to swipe aside the running mascara. I then made the mistake of dropping the visor and looking in the mirror.

"Perfect. Now I look as bad as I feel," I said to the vision of loveliness staring back at me. Bloodshot eyes, cheeks smeared with black streaks, and a red, wet nose. "Just perfect." I searched the glove compartment and came up with a lone napkin left over from some past Quarter Pounder with Cheese. Spitting on it, I rubbed the mascara off my cheeks and the snot off my upper lip. After blowing my nose on the last dry corner of the napkin, I took another deep breath, started the car, and backed out of my parking spot. Somehow I managed to reverse the multiple turns and find my way to the highway that would take me home.

The ride was excruciating. I was shaken and deeply humiliated. *I should have been more prepared.* But how could I have been? With no experience to guide me, I hadn't understood that asking the right questions in advance would have helped me understand what was expected. Then, once the meeting got rolling, I was already so freaked that there was no recovering.

The self-lashing tapered off about halfway home. I was left feeling drained and shrouded in humiliating self-doubt. I might have escaped with some semblance of pride had I not happily told everyone I knew about my upcoming meeting at Ben & Jerry's. Now I had to go home with my tail between my legs, first facing Paul and then the others. This mortifying day was going to live on and on and on. . . .

Two and a half painful hours later, I pulled the Explorer into the driveway. Two exuberant dogs greeted me at the door and I was immediately enveloped in furry, unconditional love. Wagging and smiling, they ran circles around me — ecstatic that I was home. They didn't care one whit about my failure or success.

"Thanks, guys." I buried my face in the long golden fur of Rozzi's neck. Maggie stuck her black nose under my arm and pushed her head against my chest. I held onto them for a minute, then gave each an extra treat and let them out.

I had an hour before the boys got out of school, so I started listening to messages. About halfway through I heard Santiago asking me to call him ASAP.

I dialed his number, and his receptionist, Blanca, answered.

"Lindsay, how are you?" She had a slight accent I couldn't identify. Her words were always formal and meticulously formed.

"I'm fine, thanks." *Just ducky.* "Santiago there?"

Within seconds he was on the line. "Hey there! How are you?"

Do I really have to answer that? "I'm okay. Just got home from a meeting at Ben & Jerry's that didn't go as well as I'd hoped." *If you only knew.*

"Sorry to hear that, but I have some news that's going to make you feel better."

I perked up. *Good news?* "Really?

"I had a call from Amy today." He paused.

"And?"

"She said that since No Pudge! has been off the shelves she's had so many customer complaints, she's placing another order!" His voice was triumphant.

"You're kidding?"

"And as long as the numbers stay strong, she'll keep ordering." He was as excited as I was. "She'll even continue through the summer if it keeps doing well."

"Oh, Santiago, you've made my day. No, you've made my *year*! Thank you." I had gone from the absolute depths to the tipity-top in a matter of seconds. The rush was dizzying.

"You're the one who made this happen. No Pudge! is a hit. Congratulations."

After hanging up, I treated myself to a few minutes of quiet time on the sunny patio. Owning a fledgling company was like having a toddler. Just when you think you've been pushed to the limit and are ready to collapse, the little darling does something downright brilliant. The pride you feel just sweeps your fatigue away.

"Wonder what's next," I said to the two dogs looking up at me.

I had a feeling, with two sons about to become teenagers, a still-skeptical husband and a leap-of-faith toddler pig in my life, it wouldn't be long before I'd find out.

Chapter 26

I turned the knob slowly and cracked the door as quietly as is possible in a two-hundred-year-old house. As the door groaned, Paul looked up with an annoyed, can't-you-see-I'm-on-the-phone? look.

"Sorry," I mouthed, then closed the door.

"I need to use the damn fax." I walked back down the hall to the kitchen table. The printer and fax were, of course, in his office. When he was on the road I had free rein, but when he was home, he was usually on the phone and did not want to be disturbed.

"I need to get work done, too." I sighed and glanced at my watch. Then the office door opened and, a few seconds later, the bathroom door closed. Grabbing my papers, I raced down the hall. *Gotcha!* One page after another slid through the fax in an agonizingly slow parade while I watched the second hand on my watch sweep around. *C'mon, c'mon!*

Paul wandered in, a fresh cup of coffee in his hand. "Don't you have to get the kids?"

Gee, thanks for the reminder. "I'm running a little late." Grabbing the last sheet, I headed for the garage at a run, both dogs bounding behind me.

As soon as the boys walked in the door, they headed for the refrigerator. Before the last bite reached their sweet little mouths, the daily fight over who was going to use the family computer began.

"I'm sorry, but I need to use it. You're gonna have to wait 'til after dinner."

"But Mom! I have to look some stuff up! It's for school!"

"You can do it after dinner."

"Yeah but. . ."

I employed "the Look."

The second they were out of the kitchen, I went back to my "desk" and stayed there, totally engrossed, until some hungry soul wandered into the kitchen, wondering what was for dinner. *Huh? Dinner?* Startled, I jumped up and started pulling things from the refrigerator.

By this time, the kitchen table was littered with notebooks, manila folders, phone, calculator, pens, packing tape, an empty mug, and a plate decorated with crumbs and a used tea bag. Three overflowing plastic milk-crate "filing drawers" took up floor space around my chair.

"There's no place for all this stuff," Paul muttered as he scanned the disarray, trying to find room for such foolishness as plates, forks, knives, and napkins.

I peeled, chopped, and stirred, all while watching with an eagle eye as he made messy piles that were unceremoniously dumped next to the family computer. "Be careful! I had those papers in order!"

His response to my loving reminder was either stony silence or mumbled comments such as, "I am so *bleeping* sick of all this clutter," directed into the air as if talking to himself, but just loud enough for me to hear.

The defensive little hairs on the back of my neck rose. "Where I am I supposed to work? I don't have the luxury of my own office." I won't bore you with the details of where it went from there. I'll bet you can figure it out on your own. . . .

I needed my own space. And my own computer and printer. The issue was: where?

Recently, carpenters had been turning a small bedroom off the kitchen into a dining room. When the project began, a dining room had seemed really important. But as the space changed, so did my priorities. Dining room, shmining room — the new space would be the *perfect* home for No Pudge!.

Paul wasn't exactly overjoyed. We reached a compromise. I would move No Pudge! HQ into the new space. When we had dinner guests, I would pack everything up and move it out. Desperate for my own space, I didn't think about what a pain in the ass that would be.

In June of 1997, over two years after starting No Pudge!, I moved into a kinda-sorta-all-mine real "office" complete with phone, computer, and printer.

Once the dust had settled, I scheduled a three-day visit to see my father. It appeared he'd settled happily into his new home, and I was looking forward to the first noncombative father/daughter visit in a long time.

I bunked in with Bettie and David. As soon as I unpacked, Bettie and I drove to the assisted living home. We walked down the cool, quiet hallway past the living room and through the dining room with its tables set and ready for dinner. "I was so lucky to get him in here," I said to Bettie.

She gave my arm a gentle squeeze. "Helen would have loved it."

His door was open, and as we approached, I could see him sitting in his chair with a book.

I knocked softly.

His face lit up. "Hey, sweetie." Using his walker he pushed himself to standing. "Come give your old dad a hug."

I wrapped my arms around him. He seemed less frail then the last time we'd been together. "This place is agreeing with you. You look great." His paint table and wooden easel filled a corner of the bright room.

He followed my gaze to the canvas that sat on the easel. "It's a duck-hunting piece. I think it will do well in Easton next fall," he said.

For years he and Helen had taken paintings to the annual Waterfowl Show in Easton, Maryland. I was amazed he was thinking about this year's show.

He settled back in his chair, and we spent the next hour talking about the boys, Paul, No Pudge!, and his new life. He was one of only a few male residents, a working artist, and ridiculously charming when he wanted to be, so he received vast amounts of female attention from both the residents and nurses, which was going a long way toward keeping a smile on his face. He seemed truly content.

The next day Bettie and I took him out to lunch, and he was almost cheerful. His only consistent complaints were about regimented meal times and the lack of snacks to go along with his nightly highball. After lunch we hit the grocery store and made sure his cabinets were stocked with cereal choices for a late breakfast and the cocktail peanuts and Fritos that had been the mainstay of his cocktail hour for as long as I could remember.

On my final morning, I packed my things in Bettie and David's guest room and looked out at the sun-dappled James River. For the past three days I hadn't been allowed to lift a finger — Bettie and David had spoiled me rotten. I couldn't remember the last time I had felt so cared for.

On the way to the airport, we stopped at Dad's to say goodbye.

"I won't be home 'til late so I won't call you tonight." I stood up to leave.

"There's no need for you to call every night, honey. Just check in a couple of times a week. That would be plenty."

Works for me. "Okay, if you're sure." I leaned in for a hug. "I'll be back in September once the boys are back in school." I held my cheek against his before giving him a kiss.

The last time I spoke to him was six weeks later on a midsummer afternoon. I was standing in my laundry room folding clothes still warm from the dryer when the phone rang. I was surprised to hear his voice. He rarely called, and I immediately worried something was wrong. It wasn't. He just wanted to chat. For ten minutes we talked about the boys, the gorgeous New England summer he was missing so much, and how his painting was coming along. "I love you," I told him before we hung up. "I'll give you a call in a couple of days."

The next afternoon the administrator from the assisted living home called. "It appears your father's had a stroke," she said. "We transferred him to the hospital by ambulance."

I immediately called Bettie and David and asked them to go to the hospital. Two hours later the phone rang.

"It's not good," Bettie said. "I think you'd better get down here."

My sister and I flew in the next morning. If not for his trim mustache, the gaunt, gray face on the pillow would have been almost unrecognizable. I leaned over and stroked his cheek, then put my lips close to his ear. "It's okay, Dad. I'm here," I whispered. "You can let go." A few hours later, our father quietly passed away. It was almost eight months to the day after Helen had died.

Chapter 27

One morning a few weeks before my father died, I'd been sitting in my office when my friend Gail called. She told me that QVC, the home shopping network, was planning a live show in New Hampshire. They'd asked her office to help get the word out that they were looking for new and interesting products for the show.

The first juicy quiver of excitement started to dance along the back of my shoulders.

She said since QVC had hit the airwaves in '86, it had been introducing little-known products on-air and, sometimes, selling millions of dollars worth. With the new QVC.com, the potential for a big killing was even better. They were holding auditions the following week. She finished with "I think No Pudge! would be perfect."

I wholeheartedly agreed, and headed to the auditions armed with packages of No Pudge! and baked brownies. Even though only a tiny percentage of items hit big, every person there was absolutely, positively convinced that his or her product was the next big discovery. When I received the news that No Pudge! had been accepted for the show, I was sure this was my big break.

Who needs Ben & Jerry's? I'm gonna be a star on QVC and make millions! I let the whatif happy fantasies run rampant — until the reality of working with such a monster company began to set in.

If working out the details with Traders Joe's had felt like a marathon, dealing with QVC was the equivalent of an Iron Man Triathlon. Mountains of paperwork came first, then costly custom packaging and finally the ultimate shockeroo — I'd have to sell a ton of mix just to break even. My fingers cramped trying to put a positive spin on the numbers coming out of my calculator, but the damn thing wouldn't lie. No matter how I plugged those dollar amounts in, the results consistently sucked.

"You'd have to sell how much to break even?" Bob's eyebrows arched high above his glasses in disbelief.

"But they'll be millions of viewers!" I couldn't let go of the vision that they'd all become certified No Pudge! addicts.

Jay leaned back in his chair, a small smile turning up the corners of his mouth. "Go ahead. The more you sell, the faster you'll go out of business. No problem. . ."

You may not have picked this up yet, but I can be incredibly pigheaded (no pun intended). I was gonna do this show and make it work. I mean, this was QVC! Star maker! Millionaire maker! Tens of thousands of women would dive for their phones when they realized No Pudge! was the answer to their chocolate dreams.

I'd knock 'em dead and prove Bob and Jay wrong in one fell swoop.

The Big Day — the live show in Portsmouth, New Hampshire — was scheduled for Tuesday, September 9. The day after I returned from my father's funeral.

Because of the funeral, I was excused from a mandatory seminar on Monday. No one was going to dispute that attending my father's funeral was a tad more important than "How to Sell Product on QVC." The most important thing I needed to know, they said, was that I had to demonstrate something while on the air. That was easy — adding the yogurt and mixing the batter would be the perfect demonstration. I figured the audience should sample while I mixed and stirred, so after I got home Monday night, I stayed up 'til the wee hours baking brownies.

On the Big Day, I packed the car and headed east to the New Hampshire coast. I'm not sure why no one tagged along to watch my big television debut, but I went alone. Paul and the kids would be watching from home.

When I pulled up to the theater, an ABC News van was taking up most of the curb. I maneuvered the car into a tight space on the narrow street and, balancing trays of baked brownies, made my way through the lobby and into the theater.

Large cameras dominated the stage and a tangle of wires covered the floor around them like black snakes. Spotlights roamed the walls while a woman stood center stage and repeated "Test, two, three, four — test, two, three, four," over and over as the volume of her voice rose and fell.

A QVC lady, clipboard in hand and pencil behind ear, told me to find whatever space I could backstage for my stuff. I did as I was told, then hung out in the lobby with the other wannabe millionaires. We had an hour before the doors opened to the public. People exchanged names and nervous chatter, but I kept to myself; my head felt foggy and a headache was creeping up the back of my neck. All I really wanted to do was go home, put on my pj's, and crawl into bed.

A few minutes before the doors opened, they herded us into the front rows for a last-minute pep talk, then read out the order we'd be shown in. I was near the end. *Shit. I'm gonna be here forever.*

The noise level suddenly rose as the public poured down the aisles, filling the theater seats. I felt the first butterfly come alive and start flitting around in my stomach.

Then a tall, handsome man in sharply creased khakis and button-down shirt accompanied a pert blonde in a cream-colored suit and red stiletto heels onto the stage. They must have been well-known QVC on-air personalities, because people whooped and hollered and clapped their little hearts out.

Hey, I'm gonna be a star too. Save some of that enthusiasm for the Brownie Queen!

When their moment in the spotlight arrived, most presenters maintained their composure and, prompted by the host, spoke intelligently and enthusiastically about their product. One guy, in what I guessed was an attempt to appear passionate, jumped, yelled, gesticulated wildly, and generally made an ass of himself. The woman host in her stilettos kept a safe distance. One poor woman walked onstage into the lights and froze. The male host made a joke and gently walked her to the front of the stage. She managed to eke out a few words, but her eyes were full-moon wide the entire time.

One presenter after another rolled across the stage until it was my turn. With a gentle nudge from a backstage worker, I carried my bowl, bag of mix, container of yogurt, and trusty wooden spoon on to the stage. The lights were blindingly bright. When I reached the table at the front of the stage, I was startled to see only inky blackness where audience faces should be.

Looking into the camera as I'd been told, I smiled, poured the mix into the bowl, and added the yogurt. Although the nice QVC host-man kept up a running commentary, I was so focused on smiling and stirring and smiling and mixing that I lost sight of the fact that all those ladies sitting in their living rooms, just looking for an excuse to give their credit card number to some nice operator, didn't give a flying fig how easy the brownies were to make. They just wanted to know how they tasted.

QVC host-man: "These brownies don't taste fat-free, huh?"

Brownie Queen: "Not at all — they're fudgy and rich. They just happen to be fat-free. But they're so easy to make! You want to mix until the batter is smooth and shiny — just like this!"

The director gave a hand signal. My television debut was over. The backstage folks were ready with "Good job, good job" as they helped me take off the mike, but the realization that I'd blown it was already starting to take hold.

The other wannabes had settled back into their seats after their command performances, but I quietly gathered my gear and slipped out the stage door. As I trudged down the alley, I passed the ABC correspondent getting ready for her spot on the eleven o'clock news. *Want to interview the Brownie Queen? Didn't think so. . .*

I tossed my stuff into the back of the car, poured my weary body into the driver's seat, and headed home. As much as I wanted to pretend the evening had never happened, while I wound my way through the empty, narrow streets, I couldn't help but review my performance.

Great — they're easy to make. So freakin' what? Scrambled eggs are easy to make, too. You wouldn't spend $19.95 plus shipping to buy a couple of scrambled egg mixes.

By the time I hit the highway, the self-flagellation was over. I was simply too tired to care all that much. Instead of focusing on my failed television debut, I thought about how much I had to be grateful for.

Adam's middle school experience had been less than stellar, but he was excited about making a new start at the private parochial high school he'd be starting in a couple of weeks. A.J. was a social being who believed that as long as you had friends and a place to shoot hoops, life was good. Paul and I were making strides in the sorta-kinda right direction. My move into the dining room seemed to have eased the in-your-face stress. He'd even helped me shop for my new, way-too-expensive-not-sure-how-I'm-gonna-pay-for-it computer and printer. When we arrived home, he'd unloaded, unpacked, and gotten them both up and running in no time. Now, if that isn't love, I don't know what is. We had a ways to go, but our 800-pound companion spent most of his time in the shadows, and lately he disappeared for days at a time.

Maybe No Pudge! wasn't shooting skyward on the backs of Ben & Jerry or QVC, but for a one-woman company, it was doing pretty darn well. *Maybe there is no silver bullet. Maybe I'm just gonna have to work my ass off.*

The house at the corner of our dirt road was settled into darkness for the night. I assumed that our house would be the same, but light poured from the first floor of our sprawling old cape. As I pulled into the driveway, Paul was outlined in the kitchen's glow. I saw him heading for the back door and my heart swelled. In that moment all was right with the world.

Bull. All I could think was: *Good, someone to help me unload all this crap.* As I turned off the car, I felt pretty sure, given a good nights sleep, that there wasn't anything up ahead I couldn't handle.

Ignorance is bliss.

Chapter 28

October made way for the chills of November and No Pudge!'s first exposure in the national press. In July, a woman from *Teen* magazine had called after her sister told her about the brownies. Intrigued, she thought the magazine might consider doing a review. Would I be willing to send her information and samples?

Of course!

When I called to follow up, she said the brownies had been a hit, and they might run something in a future issue. That was the last I heard from her.

Then one day in mid-October, I pulled a large manila envelope with *Teen* Magazine and a New York City return address from our p.o. box. I stood in the middle of our small, rural post office and ripped it open. Inside was a copy of the November issue of *Teen* with a post-it note marker. I immediately flipped open to the marked page. My cute, smiling pig stared up at me.

"Oh my God!"

Behind the counter, the postmaster looked up. "Everything okay?"

"Look!" I walked across the scarred wooden floor, laid the magazine down on the worn Formica, and we both leaned in.

Beneath a picture of my three bags of mix (production of Mint hadn't started until August) was the bold caption "**hot brownie**." The three-sentence blurb that followed included a line that sent tingles up my spine. "No Pudge! Brownies, the best fat-free treats we've ever tasted. . ."

"Doesn't get much better than that." A broad smile lit up Chuck's face. "One of these days, I'm going to be able to say I knew you when," he teased. "I think you're on your way."

"Yeah, on my way home." I carefully slid the magazine back into the manila envelope, placed it on top of the pile of mail and turned towards the door. "See you tomorrow, Chuck!" I attempted a nonchalant wave, but the grin was still plastered on my face, and he knew it.

At home, I walked into Paul's office and casually placed the open magazine on the desk in front of him.

"What am I looking at?" he asked.

I pointed to the picture, then waited while he silently read the few lines.

"Awesome." He flipped over to the cover. "Is this a national magazine?"

"Yup. Not bad, huh?"

"Not bad at all." He turned back to his computer. "Let's hope it translates into sales."

I picked up the magazine. "Here's the rest of your mail. You coming out for lunch?"

"Be there in a minute."

I walked down the hall towards the kitchen. I knew he'd been impressed and I also knew I was chipping away at his resistance and doubt. Trader Joe's, business growing, national magazine coverage. Chip, chip, chip.

Christmas came and the New Year, as it has a tendency to do, followed close behind. *Welcome 1998! A nice steady year without too many surprises would be great, if you can arrange it, please.* I didn't have to wait very long to find out that my request had been completely ignored.

Monday, January 5, was the first day back to school after Christmas break. I dropped Adam off at 6:25 a.m., so he could carpool to his private school in Concord with another parent. At 8:00 I unloaded A.J. and our neighbor Win at the middle school and headed home.

I don't know whether local forecasters weren't paying attention to what was happening in eastern Canada and upstate New York, or whether the ice storm devastating those areas was supposed to go around us, but no one seemed to have a clue about what was heading our way.

It started to rain around noon. I was working in my new office, paying little attention to what was happening outside. But when I heard what sounded like pebbles hitting the windows, I tuned back in. *Uh oh.* Where I live, snow is no big deal. Even a significant blizzard doesn't throw anyone off their game for long. But freezing rain and ice? Completely different.

I walked into the kitchen and looked through the sliding glass doors. The brick patio was starting to shine with an icy glow. *Damn. I wonder what it's doing in Concord.*

A year earlier, Sue and her family had moved to Concord, and they now lived a short drive from the high school where their son Kevin was a freshman with Adam.

I dialed her number.

"Hey, it's me." I said when she picked up the phone. "What's the weather doing there?"

"Raining. Why, what's it doing there?"

"Freezing rain. It's already starting to stick."

"Yuck. You want Adam to stay here tonight?"

"I might. Lemme call you back."

I had no sooner hung up the phone than Paul walked into the kitchen. "Sounds like it's icing out there. What're you gonna do about the kids?"

The phone rang. It was our neighbor. "I just got word they're closing school. I'm leaving now to pick-up Win and A.J."

I turned to Paul. "One kid taken care of. And Sue offered to keep Adam overnight."

He looked out at the gleaming patio. "Unless he wants to skate home, I think that might be a really good idea."

It rained ice all afternoon, through the night, and the entire next day. Adam stayed at Sue's that night. And the next. And the one after that. In fact, he was their guest for seven nights, while we got hit with the ice storm to end all ice storms.

We lost power during the night on Monday and wouldn't get it back for seven days. At bedtime on Tuesday, we dragged a mattress into our room for A.J., layered the beds with down comforters and two dogs, and snuggled down for the night. In the wee hours, the wind started to blow, and we were awakened by what sounded like gunshots reverberating through the woods around our old farmhouse. It took a few minutes of lying in the cold dark before we realized that the weight of the ice, combined with the strong wind, was literally snapping trees as if they were toothpicks. It was unnerving and heartbreaking.

On Wednesday, the sun came out. Downed wires and trees crisscrossed the road. Ironically, both Paul and our neighbor had just invested in small generators and so we were the only two families in the area with hot water. Our homes became shower-and-potluck central.

An adventure, sure, and even fun at times, but in the back of my mind the old whatifs were brewing. What if Adam had needed me for something? What if we hadn't known someone he could stay with? What if this happens when Adam is older and has a car and is driving himself up and down Route 89? In a couple of years A.J. would join his brother at Brady. What if he and A.J. are driving together and the weather gets bad? All I could think about was how far away we were. And how the driving conditions could change in the blink of an eye.

I kept my thoughts to myself. Paul loved our old house and the surrounding land, loved the hours he spent each fall hand-splitting cords of wood to keep the home fires burning, loved riding the old lawn mower around the three acres of grass surrounding the house. One of his favorite things was cooking Sunday morning breakfasts for family and overnight guests on the huge, almost-antique workhorse of a restaurant stove the previous owner had installed twenty years earlier. I'd often heard him jokingly say that the only way he was leaving this place was "feet first." I knew his attachment to "The Farm," as we referred to our house and its thirty-two acres, was far deeper than was either mine or the boys', and the word "move" would not be one he'd want to hear. But . . . these were our kids. They'd be traveling forty-five minutes each way on a major highway in a 3,000-pound vehicle made of flimsy metal and glass. They would run late, they would speed — this I already knew. Throw in the highway traffic and weather and my blood ran cold. But move? Was I overreacting? I had a feeling Paul would think so.

I had this conversation with myself at least ten times a day. I was driving me crazy. One night while Paul was still downstairs watching TV, I crawled into bed and lay staring at the ceiling. *What should we do?* One minute I thought I knew and the next I was totally unsure.

I closed my eyes and, without thinking, started to whisper. "God, please help me. I know a move would be hard, and I know Paul really loves it here, but I'm worried about my kids. Please tell me what to do. Thank you. Amen."

Praying for guidance wasn't something I did very often. When I did send anything heavenward, it was usually a quick thanks, unless I needed something big — like being kept alive through a fluttering-heart episode or a rollercoaster plane ride. This was different. I was looking for direct guidance and had no expectation either way as to whether I'd get an answer or if so, how.

I lay there for a quiet minute, then rolled onto my side and was asleep in seconds.

When my eyelids flickered open the next morning, the numbers on the alarm clock glowed in the darkness: 5:14. I hit the off button, then stretched and rolled over to get out of bed. My feet were halfway to the cold floor when the realization of what was rolling through my brain brought me fully and completely awake. *We have to move.*

I sat there for a moment, barely aware of the cold seeping through my toes. *What just happened?*

Whattya mean "what just happened?" Your prayer got answered.

Yeah but. . .

Yeah but nothing.

Yeah but that's never happened to me before.

Sure it has. Lots of times.

I stood up, stuck my feet in my slippers, and padded across the floor to the bathroom, the certainty of what I *knew* accompanying me. *We have to move* repeated over and over in my head. I felt no doubt, no uncertainty of any kind. The weight of the unmade decision that had been sitting on my shoulders was gone.

It was my turn to drive the crew of kids to Concord. On the way home, all I could think about was the conversation I had to have with Paul. *Do this gently, Lindsay. No rushing in like a bull in a china shop. Take it slow. Allow discussion.*

Right. Got it.

When I got home, both dogs greeted me at the door and I leaned down to rub a black belly and scratch behind a soft, golden ear. "Daddy in his office?" I murmured. Two sets of liquid brown eyes stared at me intently. I straightened up. "Might as well get this over with, huh?" Seeming to agree, both turned and trotted down the hall ahead of me. I tapped lightly on Paul's door and opened it a crack.

"Hey," he said, glancing up. "Thought I heard you come in." He picked up his mug and took a long sip, once again intent on his computer. "How was the drive?" he asked absently.

"Uneventful." I sat down in the chair next to his desk and took a deep breath. "We need to talk."

"Uh oh." He put the mug down and turned to face me. "What'd I do?" The half-concerned, half-annoyed tone really said "Now what?"

I smiled and shook my head. "You didn't do anything." Another deep breath. *How do I lead into this? Remember — take it slow. Open it up for discussion.*

"We have to move." I blurted. *Oh good. That's taking it slow.*

His eyebrows shot up. He stared at me in disbelief. "Excuse me?" He couldn't have been more stunned if I'd told him I was pregnant.

Then the rest poured out. Adam driving. The weather. Both kids in one car. The highway. Living too far away to know their friends. Driving home late on weekend nights. Things I hadn't even thought about came springing to the surface and poured out. When I was finally done he leaned back and looked at me for a long minute.

"I thought we'd be here forever," he said.

"I know you did." My heart ached for him. "I'm sorry. It's just . . . these are our kids."

"I know." He nodded slowly. "You're right."

I had expected resistance, but his face only registered sadness, and when he straightened his shoulders and turned back to his computer, his voice was firm. "Put the house on the market, it's time to move."

Chapter 29

"Thank you." I took the folder with the room key from the desk clerk and smoothly slid my business credit card into my wallet, perfectly playing the role of the professional businesswoman checking into a big-city hotel. "I have packages waiting for me," I said evenly. "I'd like to pick them up in half an hour."

It was late June and I was in New York City for No Pudge!'s first, on-its-own-like-a-big-company Fancy Food Show. At the Philadelphia show two years earlier, I'd been part of a large distributor's booth. This time No Pudge! had its own booth. It was a giant step for my little company and just below the surface of my calm, cool performance was an excited, jump-up-and-down kid.

The first step towards this day had come in March. At about the same time I'd been signing a listing agreement to put the house on the market, I was also signing an exhibitor contract committing myself to spend over two thousand dollars for a booth. I hoped I wouldn't be packing and moving when show time rolled around.

A couple of weeks later, when the exhibitor packet arrived, I discovered that paying for the 10' x 10' booth was only the beginning. One table, two chairs, and a plastic wastebasket were the only things included. Want extra lighting? A higher table? A drape around the base of the table? Stools? Carpet? Padding to go under the carpet? All extra and all very expensive. I was playing in the Big Leagues now, and it was gonna cost me.

I'd ordered one high table and carpet — no padding. I'd carry the baked samples with me on the plane, and everything else would be shipped via UPS.

A few weeks before the show, a couple from California spent over an hour looking in every corner of our old farmhouse and another hour walking the land. I feared a move/show conflict might rear its ugly head. When they returned to California without making an offer, I breathed a sigh of disappointment laced heavily with relief.

During the days leading up to the show, I made long lists of everything I might need in New York and then printed, stapled, stacked, packed, and checked off. At night I lay awake counting trade show necessities instead of sheep, wondering what crucial something I was forgetting. The Tuesday before the show I crammed three large boxes with everything from packing tape, stapler, and extra staples to bags of mix, table cloths, and sample cups. I'd bought a special shipping case for my tabletop signs and had a long shipping container made for the big banner that would hang at the back of the booth.

Show management had sent instructions for shipping directly to the Jacob Javits Center, but I worried my five small pieces would get lost in that enormous space and decided it was safer to ship everything to my hotel. Tuesday afternoon I watched the big brown truck carry my three boxes and two shipping cases down the road in a cloud of gravel and dust.

I asked my niece to come with me to New York. A pretty, thirty-year-old blonde with a ready smile and an outgoing personality, she had the ability to talk to anyone and everyone, and I thought a free weekend in the Big Apple — albeit a working weekend — would be fun for her. Unfortunately, by the time the show rolled around she was newly pregnant, constantly tired, and frequently nauseous. To add insult to injury, she was limping around in a large knee brace as a result of recent surgery.

Being a trooper, Kim insisted she still wanted to come, but now that we were here I wondered if she was having second thoughts. We'd been up since dawn to take an early shuttle from Boston to New York, and when we pulled up in front of the hotel after the typical, crazy cabbie ride from the airport, her face was a pale shade of Kermit-the-Frog green.

I'd nodded to the bellman to take our luggage, then firmly taken her arm. "Let's get you inside where it's cool." Steering her around the large lobby, I found a cushy chair in a corner and gave her a gentle shove. "Sit. I'll check in and be right back." Without a word, she'd collapsed into the soft chair, leaned her head back and closed her eyes.

As I stood at the hotel desk waiting for the clerk to check on my packages, I looked over at her. It was eleven o'clock in the morning on our first day and I was pretty sure visions of a soft bed and fluffy pillows were already dancing in her head. As soon as I finished arranging the package delivery, we'd head up to our room and settle in. I hoped a brief rest period would revive her, and then we'd be off to the Javits to set up.

"Let me see what we have for you Mrs. Frucci," the desk clerk murmured, her long, red fingernails clicking away at her keyboard. She scanned the screen. Frowning, she clicked a couple more times. "Could the packages be under another name?"

My stomach lurched. "They shouldn't be, but you could try No Pudge."

Her heavily lined eyes swiveled from the computer screen to my face. "No Pudge?" she repeated as if she hadn't heard me correctly.

"Yes. N-O-space-P-U-D-G-E. No Pudge. But I sent them to my attention here, with the check-in date right on the label." The knot in my belly tightened. "There are five packages and they should have been delivered Thursday. Yesterday at the latest."

She clicked a couple more times, scanned her computer again and shook her head. "I don't see anything."

"That's not possible." Calm and cool was rapidly being replaced by freaked out and twitching. *This can't be happening. This cannot be happening.*

She seemed to get that I was on the verge of panic and reached for her phone. An out-of-control woman at the front desk was something to avoid at all costs.

"Let me call shipping," she said in her most soothing, please-don't-get-hysterical voice. Someone answered the phone and she explained why she was calling. She looked at me and smiled reassuringly, "He's checking."

I nodded mutely. *Be there, be there, be there, be there.*

She focused intently on her computer while she listened. Finally she turned to me. "I'm sorry, Mrs. Frucci. Nothing has been delivered either under your name or No Pudge."

I just stared at her, frozen, speechless.

She waited a heartbeat or two, then not-so-subtly glanced behind me at the next person in line. Numbly I turned and started across the lobby to where Kim was slumped in her chair.

I was about to race through all Five Stages of Grief in rapid succession. Stage One? Denial. I was so there. *I can fix this. I've worked too hard and planned too long and this is my first show and they'll turn up.*

Kim looked up. "What's wrong?"

I told her and the resulting look of disbelief and horror on her face must have mirrored my own.

"What're we gonna do?"

"We're going to our room and I'm gonna call UPS. They'll just have to find the boxes and get them here. Period."

"WHAT DO YOU MEAN YOU CAN'T DO ANYTHING UNTIL MONDAY?" Okay, so maybe they weren't going to find them and get them here.

I was sitting at the desk in our hotel room, holding the phone in a death grip. Kim and the bellman, who'd arrived with our two suitcases and the three coolers containing all my baked samples, stood in the background listening as my voice rose. I was talking to — or rather yelling at — a UPS supervisor.

I'd moved on to the second Stage of Grief — Anger. When the unfortunate customer-service representative who'd initially picked up my call blithely told me there was "nothing we can do," I'd gone ballistic. Sensing she had a crazy person looking for someone to kill on the other end of the phone, she'd opted for self-preservation and rapidly handed me off to her supervisor. I was now screaming at one of those thick-skinned, unflappable people who, in their role as Customer Service Supervisor, deal with hysterically pissed off customers every day.

"I am terribly sorry, Mrs. Frucci," he was saying for the two or three hundredth time. "If there was something I could do to help you, I would, but I can't do anything until Monday. Our distribution center is closed for the weekend." His tone had not wavered one octave since getting on the line.

The sounds coming out of my mouth, on the other hand, had been steadily climbing in both pitch and volume. "How can it be closed? UPS does Saturday deliveries!"

"Those deliveries are done in the morning. The distribution center closes at noon."

I looked at my watch. It was 11:50. I decided to try honey instead of vinegar. "Listen," I wheedled sweetly, "it's ten minutes before twelve. Couldn't you just call and ask them to look? *Please?*" Moving on to the third

Stage of Grief — Bargaining. Or, in my case — begging. I was certain my packages were sitting in a warehouse somewhere in Manhattan and my predicament could be quickly solved if someone would just *look.* "I don't think you understand, if I don't get those boxes, it could mean the end of my business." A rather dramatic overstatement, but I was playing my only-you-can-rescue-poor-little-me card.

He wasn't moved.

I finally gave up, hung up, and dropped my head into my hands.

"I'm so sorry, Auntie Lin." Kim's voice barely penetrated the gloom.

I sat up, leaned back in the chair, and stared out the window. The blue sky and a few passing clouds reflected off the glass windows of the building directly across 54th Street. The colors began to liquefy and run together as my eyes filled with tears. I'd officially landed in Stage Four — Sadness. My shoulders slumped. I picked up the phone again. "I'll call Paul and tell him we're coming home." And she sprints across the finish line to Stage Five — Acceptance!

The poor guy answered the phone with a cheery, "Hey, how's everything in the Big Apple?"

You're about to wish you hadn't asked that question. When I told him, he was stunned. "Whad'ya gonna do?"

"I'm thinking we'll hang around for a night so I can get good and drunk. Kim will be my designated walker — or gimper — and then she can pour my sad, hung-over body onto the plane in the morning."

"There really isn't any way you can do the show?"

"I have the baked samples but I don't have anything else. I don't even have bags of mix. Everything was in those boxes." Deep sigh and long sniffle.

"This really sucks," he paused, as if searching for something encouraging to say. "I'm sorry, honey. You worked so hard to get ready for this."

"I'll call the airlines and call you back when I know what we're doing." I managed.

"Okay. Love you."

"I know. I love you too."

As soon as I hung up the phone, Kim hobbled over. "Um, I don't know if this helps in any way," she said, "but the bellman knows where the distribution center is." She handed me a piece of paper with an address. "He says it's not far from the convention center."

A glimmer of desperate hope rekindled. "What the hell." I looked at her. "You up for another cab ride?"

"Absolutely." Like I said, she was a trooper. "Let's go."

Thirty minutes later, we were standing in the glaring sun outside a windowless brick building that took up an entire city block. Across the street, a chain-link fence surrounded a large parking lot filled with big brown trucks. It looked like we were in the right place.

We were on the west side of midtown Manhattan, only a block east of the Hudson River and about a mile and a half south of the Javits Center where, at this very minute, we were supposed to be happily setting up a booth for my very first Fancy Food Show. So near and yet so far. . .

We walked south past one huge, closed garage door after another. I hated to acknowledge it by saying it out loud, but the place did seem to be deserted. I could practically hear my packages calling from inside. "There has to be a regular door. Let's try the side street." I started moving purposefully towards the corner. "How you doin'?" I asked over my shoulder as Kim hurriedly gimped after me.

"I'm fine. Don't worry about me." Like aunt, like niece. We were both totally focused on getting into that damn fortress. Rivulets of sweat were running down my back and my bra felt like it was glued on.

"Look," I exclaimed as we rounded the corner. "The door!"

"Finally," she gasped as she came up behind me. Leaning against the warm brick wall, she took a long swallow from her water bottle.

I walked up to the glass door, grabbed the handle and pulled. Nothing. Leaning in, we cupped our hands around our eyes. On the other side of the glass we could make out a small, empty room with a desk and a couple of chairs.

"Auntie Lin — look." Kim was pointing to what appeared to be an intercom. Without hesitation, I walked over and leaned on the bell below it. We waited — grateful for the shade of the door's overhang. I was about to ring again when the door suddenly opened. A young security guard stood there.

The poor guy never had a chance. We explained why we were there and what we wanted to do. His response was a firm "No." We pleaded. He said "No" again, but this time with a smile. We cajoled. He said he ". . . really couldn't." We begged.

He raised his hands in surrender and gave in.

A determined, focused woman on a mission is about as stoppable as a runaway freight train. Just ask any man who's come up against one. Two determined women? Fuhgetaboutit.

He not only let us in, but helped us search for the five missing packages that were supposedly calling my name. We scrambled over and around boxes of every conceivable size and shape, even crawling up stationary conveyor belts, searching every corner of the biggest damn warehouse I had ever seen.

If the packages were calling, it was in a whisper. After two solid hours, I stood looking over the sea of boxes in disbelief. "They're not here." How was this possible? Getting into the warehouse was supposed to solve everything. We'd talked our way in the door and still didn't have the things needed to do the show. "I can't believe this."

The security guard walked us to the door and unlocked it. "I'm really sorry." He held the door open.

"Hey, can't say we didn't try." I smiled and held out my hand. "Thank you." He gave me a warm, firm handshake, then turned back into the cool, dark building. Kim and I walked out into the heat.

"Now what?" she asked.

I looked at her. Her cheeks were flushed and beads of perspiration dotted her upper lip. "We find a cab. I'm going to the Javits Center to check-in. You're going back to the hotel and take a nap."

She nodded. "I'm whipped."

"I know you are." I put my arm around her shoulder and gave a quick squeeze. "You've been great." We started walking. Just ahead, the river glistened in the late afternoon sun.

"I just wish we'd found them."

"Me too."

Chapter 30

I had no idea what I hoped to accomplish at the Javits, but I'd done all this planning and come all this way — I felt like I should at least set foot in the door.

After checking in, I walked onto the show floor. It was the usual chaotic set-up-day scene. Weaving my way around huge wooden crates and empty cardboard boxes, I finally came to the space I'd been assigned. A piece of thin gray carpet covered the concrete floor. Two tables, two folding plastic chairs and a rubber wastebasket waited forlornly in the middle.

Standing in the aisle, I tried to envision what it might have looked like if my boxes had arrived. And then I made the mistake of scanning the booths around me. In the double booth to my left, custom lighting gave the space a warm glow and highlighted strategically-placed display pedestals. Glass shelves were filled with elegant packages and a cushy burgundy carpet covered the floor. I couldn't have competed with that, no matter how many boxes I had.

I walked back into my sad little booth. Almost without thought, I started moving the tables and chairs around until it was organized the way I'd envisioned it. Once again, I stepped out into the aisle. My brain began to hum. *You know, maybe, just maybe. . .* I glanced at my watch — official show rules stated that all booths had to be set up by five p.m. It was 4:15. I grabbed my purse, leaving my bare booth behind.

I quickly found a table manned by an official-looking older gentleman and explained my predicament. "If you can pull it together before the show opens at ten tomorrow morning," he told me, "you'll be fine." The doors opened for exhibitors at eight. I'd have two hours to set up.

A silky tingle of adrenaline started replacing the hair shirt of woe I'd been wearing all afternoon.

When I walked into the hotel room twenty minutes later, Kim's eyes fluttered open. She stretched and yawned. "That nap was just what I needed." She sat up, propped the pillows against the headboard, and leaned back. "So, how was it?"

"You're not gonna believe it, but I think we just might be able to pull this off." I grabbed my briefcase and started rummaging through it. "We have the one thing we couldn't do without — the baked samples." I pulled out a sell sheet and order form and held them up triumphantly. "And I have these, so I can make copies. We can improvise the rest." I plopped in a chair, kicked off my shoes, and wiggled my poor, tired toes. "The only thing I haven't figured out is how to get bags of mix. No Pudge! isn't in any stores here yet, so we can't just go out and buy a few bags."

"How about we ask Uncle Paul to ship some overnight via UPS?" We both laughed.

"The nearest store is probably the Trader Joe's in Darien, Connecticut, but we don't have any way to get there."

Kim perked right up. "Val lives in Darien! I'll call her and see if she can bring us some."

Val and Kim were close friends, but it was six o'clock on Saturday night and we needed the mix by ten the next morning — at the latest. Darien was an hour's drive without traffic.

"I don't know, that's an awful lot to ask."

But Kim was already reaching for the phone on the bedside table.

"If she's around —" she dialed the number "— she'll do it." She was quiet for what seemed like an eternity, then looked at me. "Answering machine."

Shit.

She left a message saying she was in New York and had a huge favor to ask. Would Val please call as soon as she got in? She hung up the phone and moved to the edge of the bed. "Don't worry, she'll call."

"I hope so. We don't have any other options."

"She'll call." There was that absolute certainty again. I desperately wanted to believe her and simply accepted her conviction, as she'd accepted mine that UPS would find and deliver the packages. The fact I'd been wrong was conveniently forgotten.

"I just have to pee and brush my teeth, then I'll be ready to roll!" Leaning down, she grabbed her knee brace from the floor. "So what else do we have to do?" she asked as she strapped the contraption on her leg.

"We need to go shopping and then we need to get some food."

"Good!" Brace in place, she hopped off the bed and headed for the bathroom. "I'm starving!"

We spent the next couple of hours running around buying tablecloths, plates, paper napkins, plastic knives, wet wipes, and a stapler. It was far from all the stuff packed in my three boxes, but I hoped it would be enough to get us through.

Back at the hotel, we threw our loot on the bed and checked for messages. Nothing. I called room service for dinner so we could stay close to the phone. My hopes were rapidly dwindling.

Five minutes after placing our order, Val called.

Sure, the darling, wonderful girl said, she'd be happy to go to Trader Joe's and buy mix. She'd also drive it into the city early the next morning.

I looked at my watch — 8:30. "They close at nine," I grinned. "We just made it."

But by the time Val got there, the doors were locked. When she knocked on the glass, an employee shook his head and mouthed the word "Closed."

At the time she was working for one of the major television networks and in an absolutely brilliantly, albeit slightly dishonest, though totally understandable-given-the-circumstances move, she reached into her bag and pulled out her network I.D. Holding it against the glass, she banged again. When the employee saw the network logo, he grabbed the manager, and they immediately came to the door. On the spot she created a story about forgetting to get the mix for a Sunday morning show. If she showed up without it, she'd get fired. They opened the door wide and let her buy as much as she wanted. Have I mentioned that I love this girl?

While Val's Trader Joe's scenario was playing out, Kim and I were sitting on our beds, inhaling dinner. As I stacked the empty plates, I told her I was heading back out but informed her, in no uncertain terms, that she was staying put and going to bed. She put up very little fight.

It was ten o'clock by the time I hit the still-crowded, midtown-Manhattan sidewalks and headed to Kinko's. I walked into the empty store and approached the two bored-looking guys languishing behind the counter. They looked like it would take a firecracker, carefully placed you-know-where, to get them moving. But when they heard my tale of woe, they sprang into action. While I labored at the computer, composing my signs, they copied and collated the sell sheets and order forms. Then they printed out my single-color signs on legal-sized paper. Working together, we cut pieces of cardboard from boxes and glued the paper on. In a make-you-believe-in-humankind team effort, I walked out of there at midnight with order forms, sell sheets and signs that read:

PLEASE PARDON OUR APPEARANCE
Our booth and all its contents
have disappeared into
UPS
Never-Never Land

As long as Val brought the mix, we'd be ready when the show doors opened.

When I walked onto the show floor at 8:05 the next morning, a few other exhibitors were putting finishing touches on their booths, but for the most part the hall was empty and quiet. Clear aisles, lined with freshly vacuumed, deep-red carpet had magically replaced the chaotic scene of the day before.

I reached my booth and started unloading the dolly I'd brought. An hour later, I arranged the last pile of order forms, pushed the cooler under the table, and walked into the aisle to survey my handiwork. I suddenly realized that while I had been so intent on putting my booth together, the hall had come alive.

"I just read your sign. You poor thing!" A fellow exhibitor appeared next to me, dressed in a crisp, white chef's coat. "If you need anything, I'm three booths down." With a wave, she was off.

An older couple came strolling down the aisle, wearing matching aprons printed with large strawberries. Her hand rested comfortably in the crook of his elbow. They stopped when they saw the sign. "Same thing happened to us a few years back when we were new at this." A broad Midwestern accent lilted his words. "This your first show?"

"It is."

He pulled a card out of his apron pocket and offered it to me. "Listen, we've learned a thing or two in twenty years." He looked down at the woman beside him. "Haven't we sweetheart?"

"We certainly have, dear," she nodded.

Dear Lord, it's Ozzie and Harriet. . .

"Call us anytime. We'd be happy to let you in on a few secrets we've learned along the way." He patted me on the shoulder. "Good luck!"

And so it began. News of my dilemma spread, and exhibitors began to wander over to see how I was doing, offering supplies, an endless stream of moral support, and, more important, the beginning of a list of names and contacts that would prove invaluable. "Here, write this down — I've got this great broker in Cincinnati," or "There's a small distributor that covers the Mid-Atlantic States. I think they'd love your stuff," and "I have the phone number of the buyer for the southeast region of Kroger. Tell him I told you to call."

For the first time since starting No Pudge! I felt part of a community. Just like me, these people were working their butts off to establish a brand in an industry filled with complicated twists and expensive turns, an industry where hundreds of products competed for the same limited shelf space. Every time I went to the ladies room, I changed my route, and no matter which way I went, I passed booth after booth offering salsas, sauces, spice rubs, pickles, or chocolate-covered something or other. At least my product was unique. I couldn't imagine trying to sell a buyer the fiftieth salsa he'd seen since walking in the door.

Kim made it with five minutes to spare, hobbling as fast as she could down the aisle with a large carton in her arms. We arranged the precious bags of mix on the table, and then stood back to admire our handiwork.

"You know, it doesn't look half bad," Kim said.

I nodded. "It sure isn't gonna win any beauty contest, but if they decided to hand out an award for getting creative in a pinch, I think we'd get top honors."

The doors opened and the aisles quickly jammed with buyers, their entourages, and small-store owners with families in tow. Once our bare-bones look caught their eye, they slowed down to read the sign, then came over to commiserate and try a sample.

As the day drew to a close, I looked up to see a blonde woman in a flowing tunic standing in front of me. I recognized her as the proprietor of the fancy booth next door.

"Hi," she said with a smile. "May I try one?"

"Of course!" Attendee or exhibitor — to me they were all potential No Pudge! customers.

She popped a brownie in her mouth. A smile spread across her face. "These are delicious," she said.

"Thanks."

"I can't believe how much attention you guys are getting," she continued. "I spent thousands of dollars on my booth, and you have twice the traffic! You should use the "UPS lost my booth" ploy at every show."

The beautiful booth lady was envious of *us*! All right!

Collapsed in the backseat of the cab on our way to the hotel after the show, I turned to Kim. "We're going out for a really nice dinner. We've earned it!"

"Sounds good to me." She patted her mini baby bump. "We're ravenous!"

"Yeah," I laughed. "Well, neither of you can drink, but honey, I can, and let me tell you, there's a bottle of red wine out there with my name on it!"

The next morning we were hauling a load of large, sample-filled coolers to the elevator when the doors slid open and three twenty-something women wearing show badges emerged. I may have been a trade show newbie, but even I knew that every badge was color-coded and that, at this Fancy Food Show, a brown stripe meant "Press," and "Press" meant the potential for some much-needed free advertising.

These women were wearing badges with a brown stripe. I only had a second or two as they walked by to figure out who they worked for, but their badges were easier to read than most. Just three capital letters — GMA.

Good Morning America! "Excuse me," I said as they passed us. They halted and turned. Smiling, I stuck out my hand to the closest one. *C'mon, honey, engage.*

"My name is Lindsay Frucci. I own a small company named No Pudge! Foods, and we (ah, the royal *we*) make all-natural, fat-free brownie mixes."

"Hi." "Hello." "Hey." Three barely polite, very indifferent, "we're busy" handshakes. None offered her name. After all, they worked for *Good Morning America* and I was just another lowly exhibitor.

I continued smiling warmly. *Show a little respect, I'm old enough to be your damn mother.* "I take it you're here scouting products for Good Morning America?"

Two of them looked at the tall, model-skinny brunette to my right. She nodded. "Yes, but we've already decided which products we're using."

Tough. I shifted into verbal hyperdrive. "Listen, you have to come to our booth. Our brownies are amazing —

you won't find anything else like them at the show. I promise you won't be disappointed. I mean, doesn't the idea of a fudgy, decadent brownie that just happens to be fat-free sound worth the trip?" I paused to take a breath. "Oh, and did I mention, the only thing you add to the mix is fat-free vanilla yogurt? Like I said, very unique. And they're delicious. You have to try them."

With a perfectly manicured, pink fingertip, Miss Skinny clicked her pen and held it over her notebook. "What booth did you say it was?"

I watched her write it down and as they turned to walk away I flashed a big, you-guys-are-great, smile. "See you later!" I called to their retreating backs.

Stifling a giggle, Kim held up her hand for a high-five. "Way to go, Auntie Lin!"

I smacked her raised palm. "Now let's hope they actually stop by."

A few busy hours later, I looked up to see all three girls standing in front of the booth. Miss Skinny delicately picked up a sample and took a tiny nibble.

Aw, c'mon! I wanted to yell at her. *You have to actually* taste *it!*

The other two girls tossed full samples in their mouths, started to chew, and immediately reached for seconds. "OhmyGOD, these are *so* good!" "C'mon Alison, try the whole thing. They're to die for!"

Miss Skinny, a.k.a. Alison, bravely placed the entire sample in her mouth. It was only seconds before her eyes got big, and she looked at the other two and grinned. "We're about to sit down with our boss and review everything we liked," she said to me, reaching for a second sample. "I can't guarantee anything, but. . . ." She paused to swallow.

Yes? "but" what??

"I think you have a really good shot of getting on the air. These are amazing."

Ecstatic, I loaded them up with bags of mix and said goodbye. They were walking away when, suddenly, skinny Alison turned back.

Uh oh.

"One for the road!" She flashed a bright smile as she scooped another sample from the plate, and then hurried after her co-workers.

The next morning at promptly seven a.m., Kim and I settled ourselves in front of the television. The first hour of *Good Morning America* focused on world events, political news and other such frivolous nonsense. *C'mon, c'mon — get to the good stuff!* By 8:30 I was pacing. By 8:45 I was sure they'd bagged the segment altogether.

Then Charlie Gibson announced that Sara Moulton, the show's Foods Contributor, was going to review products from this year's Fancy Food Show.

I stopped pacing and settled my butt on the edge of the bed. My stomach was doing jumping jacks.

"After the break."

We both groaned loudly.

"Could you drag this out any more?!" I yelled at the television.

Commercial finally over, the camera zoomed in on Sara standing at a table lined with goodies. We didn't have to wait long because the second one she showed was No Pudge! and she introduced it by saying, "This was our favorite product of the show." *Holy crap.* I jumped up and grabbed Kim, and we danced and whooped and hugged. My bag of No Pudge! on *Good Morning America*! I was sure this was my big break, until I realized they weren't giving out phone numbers or web addresses, and we were in so few stores that people who saw the segment and looked for No Pudge! probably wouldn't find it.

I floated on air anyway. Given how the show experience had begun and how close I had come to getting drunk and going home, the feeling was magical.

Ten days after I returned home, I looked out my office window one afternoon to see the familiar big brown truck pulling into the driveway. I walked outside in time to watch the driver unload my three boxes and two cases. *Well, whad'ya you know. . .* A bit worse for wear, but nonetheless intact, my booth for the New York Fancy Food Show had returned from Never-Never Land.

Chapter 31

Trying to get all four Fruccis in one room for more than a passing minute was no mean feat, so Paul and I had a couple of days to sweat out how to break the news that we were moving. We figured Adam would be thrilled. A.J.? Not so much. He was already miffed about our plan to send him to Bishop Brady instead of the local high school with his buddies. Throw in the news that we might be moving before he finished middle school, and we'd be in for an adolescent fit of earth-shaking magnitude.

We finally managed to corral everyone at dinner one night. Fortified with a pre-dinner glass of wine, I started. "Guys? Dad and I have something to tell you."

Two forks paused in mid-air. Two sets of dark brown eyes rimmed in long, thick eyelashes (a gift from their father) swiveled to me.

"What?"

"We've decided to put the house on the market and move to Concord." A.J.'s jaw dropped and his face began to cloud. But before he could protest, I hit him with our planned *coup de grace.* "But even if the house sells quickly, we promise you can finish eighth grade here."

His mouth closed. "Really?"

I nodded. "Really."

"Okay," he shrugged, picked up his fork and went back to his pasta.

I looked at Paul and smiled. *That went well, don't you think?* I channeled.

It did. Good job. He channeled back.

Adam's excited chatter took over and dinner progressed.

We had eighteen months to sell the house, buy a new one, and move before A.J. started his freshman year at Brady and Adam got his license. Given the remote, end-of-a-dirt-road location of our house, Paul and I figured it might easily take that long.

It didn't. The couple from California reappeared in July, and suddenly we needed a place to live for A.J.'s entire eighth-grade year.

Luckily, Sue's New London house was back on the market and empty. I contacted the owner, who was only too happy to rent it to us for the winter. It was the perfect place to hang our hats for the next ten months. Not only was it a house that Adam and I were familiar with, it also had two large home offices with multi-line phone hook-ups and cable internet connections.

The years at "The Farm" had been tumultuous, and maybe for that reason I wasn't terribly sad to be moving on. I prayed that when I pulled out of that driveway for the last time, I'd be leaving our 800-pound gorilla behind with the dust bunnies.

Within days of our move, I hired my first real employee. Wendy, who'd been with me at the FMI show in Chicago, had recently stepped back from her gourmet chocolate business, and when I asked if she'd help me with No Pudge!, she quickly agreed.

Our arrangement was loose, but worked well. During the busiest time of the day, she handled anything that didn't need my personal touch, so I could focus on the ever-demanding "Get Into More Stores" that leered from its lofty perch.

As early fall chilled into late fall, the Concord house hunt began in earnest. On a house-hunting expedition one Saturday, Paul and I discovered an undeveloped lot, tucked at the end of a windy, nine-house cul-de-sac and bordered on two sides by woods. Private, level, and only about a six-minute drive to Brady — it was perfect.

A builder we knew said the lot was owned by an abutter and not for sale, but suggested it wouldn't do any harm to contact them. I dropped a note in the mail and crossed my fingers. Within a few days, they called and said they were interested in selling. We closed in two weeks. Boom. Done. Unbelievable.

In early December, we broke ground for a simple, center-entrance colonial we dubbed "The Kid House." This was going to be the last home Adam and A.J. would know before they left for college and moved on with their lives. We wanted them to want to bring their friends home and wanted those friends to feel welcome and comfortable there.

To accommodate Paul's need for an office and my need for a No Pudge! home, we designed an oversized attached garage with finished second floor. Along with bays for two cars, the ground level would have a separate "Pack and Ship" room for No Pudge!.

During the week, our four nonstop busy schedules seemed to be in constant conflict. And it was my responsibility to keep it all straight. I was starring in my own, one-woman juggling act, and my biggest fear was that one day Adam would be left shivering in the late-afternoon gloom outside of school, waiting for his mother who was sitting in her car, forty-five minutes away, waiting for A.J., who was somewhere else entirely.

But there was an upside to all the insanity.

Naturally, Adam wanted to hang with his high-school buddies on Saturday nights. So at least a couple of weekend evenings a month Paul, A.J., and I drove him to Concord, dropped him at a friend's house, and went to dinner and a movie. At the end of the evening, we'd pick him up and all go home.

In addition, Paul and I spent every Saturday in the car, meeting with the builder and shopping for the new house.

Driving home from house-building errands one cold, blue-sky Saturday, I turned in the passenger seat to look at the familiar face I was finally starting to recognize again. "You know what?"

"No, what?"

"I like this."

"Like what?" He glanced over.

"This. Us. It feels like we're a team again."

He reached across the seat, took my hand and gave it a gentle squeeze. "Yeah, it does."

With our fingers firmly entwined, I settled back in my seat and glanced into the side mirror. No gorilla anywhere in sight.

In mid-May, a reporter from the *Wall Street Journal* called. She was doing a story on the new trend of women-launched businesses across the country. SCORE had given her my name as a possible resource. I answered her questions, and she said she'd call me if the story was going to run. I didn't hear back from her, and forgot all about it.

One early June morning, Paul hopped into a New York City cab and on the seat next to him was *The Wall Street Journal.* He scanned the first page, did a double take, and grabbed his cell phone.

"You're on the front page of the *Wall Street Journal*!"

"What?"

"Above the fold! *Lindsay Frucci founded No Pudge! Foods, a company in Elkins, NH, that makes fat-free brownie mix.* . . . This is amazing. My wife — quoted on the front page of the *Journal*!"

Apparently, throughout the rest of the day, I popped up everywhere. He walked into the lobby of a company where he had a meeting and there was the *Journal,* sitting on a table. He'd walk into someone's office and the paper stared back at him from the desk. He proudly pointed it out to everyone he met.

So, I'm on the front page of the Wall Street Journal *and suddenly I'm validated?*

Does it really matter how he gets there, as long as he does?

Good point. Works for me.

About the same time that the *Journal* reporter had called, a Weight Watcher's leader in Connecticut called to say she'd just tried the brownies.

"They're only two points!" Lucy was excited.

I had no idea what she was talking about. "I take it that's good?"

Most brownies, she said, were five or six points in the new Weight Watcher point system. Finding one for so few was very good indeed.

"*Weight Watchers* magazine needs to review these. Would you mind if I wrote to them?" she asked.

Would I mind?!

Thanks to Lucy's persistence, the September 1999 issue of *Weight Watcher's* magazine had this to say: *"If a fat-free, 2-POINT brownie that's just as fudgy as the real thing sounds too good to be true, then you haven't tried No Pudge! Brownies. . . ."*

A couple of days after the magazine hit the stands, Wendy put a call on hold and raised her eyebrows at me. "You might want to talk to this lady. She's a Weight Watcher's leader in Texas and sees six hundred members a week."

"Six hundred?!"

I picked up the phone. "Hi, this is Lindsay Frucci. Wendy tells me you're a Weight Watcher's leader?"

"Yes, ma'am. I do ten meetings a week in the Houston area and have about sixty people in each one. I was wonderin' if there's any place around here I could buy your brownies. I'd love to share 'em with my members."

My response was as automatic as if I'd planned on this call coming in for weeks. "We don't have them in any stores in Texas yet, but I'd be happy to send you a bag of each flavor for yourself and one bag to give away at each of your meetings." Just like that, the No Pudge! Weight Loss Leader Sampling Program was born.

What began as a single phone call soon became my primary marketing strategy. One leader would call, and we'd send samples. She'd tell another leader, and that leader would call. She'd e-mail three others, who would each tell two more, and so on. Each leader saw anywhere from twenty to one thousand members a week. The No Pudge! "word" was starting to spread like wildfire.

As the wildfire grew however, a new whatif fear manifested itself. Whatif a big company like Betty Crocker or Duncan Hines saw how we were growing and launched a fat-free, just-add-yogurt brownie mix of their own? They could manufacture it for less, offer it at a much lower price, spend millions marketing it, and squash me like a bug. That fear became my greatest motivator. Making No Pudge! the brand people thought of when they thought of "better-for-you brownies" was the only way to protect my fledgling company. And something told me Weight Watcher's leaders and their members might be my stairway to branding heaven.

When we moved, Wendy had agreed to stay through the summer. As the end of August and her departure drew near, I hired my first full-time, permanent employee. Linda had experience running an office and was a skilled bookkeeper. She was also a mom with pets—so working in a house with kids and dogs roaming around wasn't an issue.

For almost five years I'd been telling myself and everyone around me that I could create a business and make it work. But it wasn't until the moment I sat in my real, official office, at my real, official desk with my real, official multi-line phone, across from my real, official full-time employee, that I acknowledged I'd actually done it.

Yup, I had a solid little company that was growing like crazy. And the growing pains were just beginning.

Chapter 32

Dressed casually in khakis and a blue button-down, with slightly receding hair and an easy smile, the Hannaford buyer seemed like a nice guy. We'd settled in his office, and I was just starting to relax when he leaned back in his chair and studied me across the desk. "Do you know the cost of getting a new product on the shelf here?"

"Cost?" This was my first appointment with a big-chain grocery buyer and I didn't want to screw it up. *Is this a trick question?* I honestly still thought that if you had a good product in good packaging, people would want to buy it and the big chain stores would put it on the shelf. Ahh, the end of the innocence. . .

I shook my head.

"We typically charge $23,000 per item for the warehouse and $150 per item per store."

Twenty-three THOUSAND dollars?! Per item?!

"Really?" I managed to croak. It was remarkable I was still seated and upright.

I had just been formally introduced to "slotting": the nonrefundable security deposit that big grocery chains demand for the use of their real estate (a.k.a. shelf space). I soon learned that although slotting charges might vary from chain to chain, no matter which Big Boy you were talking to, it was going to cost megabucks just to get in the door.

His brown eyes were sympathetic. "I had a feeling this would be news."

I shrugged helplessly. "There's no way I can afford that."

He leaned forward in his chair. "Look, I can't bring your mix into the regular baking aisle, but I think you have a pretty neat product."

Whoopee.

"There may be another alternative."

I sat up straight. "Really?"

He nodded. "Our Nature's Place departments are expanding into more stores, and tend to be a lot looser with these requirements. No Pudge! might be a good fit there." He paused with a crooked smile. "Would you like me to talk to the buyer?"

By early summer, all four flavors of No Pudge! were on the shelves in the Nature's Place section of every Hannaford Brothers. It hadn't cost me a penny.

But for the first time, I'd come face to face with the costly demands of big distributors and major grocery chains, and the idea of going up against these guys terrified me. On the other hand, I was desperate to get into more stores. I'd gotten into Bread & Circus and Hannaford's natural foods section without paying slotting, so maybe targeting the natural-food sections cropping up in other big grocery chains was the way to reach my goal without going broke. With that in mind, I called the natural-foods buyer at Shaw's Supermarkets and wangled an appointment. On a gorgeous late-spring day, I made the two-hour trek to Bridgewater, Massachusetts.

The buyer was a friendly guy in a rumpled suit. I put the plate of brownies on his desk, and he immediately took one. As I told him how well the mixes were doing at Bread & Circus and Hannaford, the brownie disappeared. He reached for another. "So, Lindsay," he washed down his last bite with a slug of coffee. "I think these will do well for us."

"Great!"

"We'll need two cases per item per store for slotting."

So much for being more reasonable in the natural section. At least this time, I hadn't been completely blindsided. "Al," I looked him in the eye. "No Pudge! is a tiny, two-woman company. I can't afford that." Without fully realizing it, I'd just drawn a line in the sand.

"Okay," he nodded. "I understand."

That was easy.

"How about one case?"

Or not.

I took a deep breath. I desperately wanted to say yes. I wanted this business — this was Shaw's! It would be a really big step.

You can't.

"Al, I can't." *This sucks. Right decision but it sucks.*

"Lindsay, c'mon." Al spread his hands in supplication. "You have to give me something! There's no way I can bring this in without something."

"I'm sorry. It would be irresponsible of me to commit to something I can't afford. I just can't." Defeated, I bent down and put my notebook in my briefcase then looked up at him. "But you've been really nice. Thank you for your time." I started to rise.

"Okay. Sit down, you win."

Huh? I win? I fell back in my seat and stared at him.

He was smiling broadly. "Hey, it's a great product and it's unique. I think it'll do really well."

What just happened? "It will. You won't regret this. Thank you."

"So," he said, jotting down notes on a paper on his desk as he continued talking. "We'll want to bring this in through Millbrook." Millbrook, one of the largest grocery distributors in the Northeast, wasn't even on my radar screen, and I sure as hell wasn't on theirs.

"I'm not in Millbrook." *Is this going to kill it?*

He looked up and smiled again. "You are now. If I want them to take you, they will."

I walked out on air. I was in Shaw's. And Millbrook! I had drawn my line in the sand, stuck to it, and won.

But as the year drew to a close, the glow from my two conquests faded. Even with the addition of Hannaford and Shaw's, Trader Joe's West Coast stores were the only place outside of New England where people could find my mixes. And Trader Joe's accounted for 80 percent of our total sales. Both Amy and Karen seemed happy with how things were going, but if something changed, and they decided to drop the mix, I was in deep trouble.

I was working too damn hard for too little gain. Although I didn't have the funds or the desire to take on the Big Boys' costly little system, I had to face the fact that distribution was expanding very slowly. I'd have to either jump off the going-after-national-distribution cliff or be content with No Pudge! staying a small, regional company.

Accepting regional status without making the effort to grow was simply not an option. I had not gone through the turmoil of the last four years to stop now. The time had come to jump. Either my parachute would open and I'd grow the business, or I'd crash and burn. At this point, either scenario seemed preferable to the slow road to Grocery Outer Mongolia I was currently creeping along.

The successes at Hannaford and Shaw's had given me just enough confidence to take my show on the road. The upcoming distributor show in Palm Springs was the perfect first stop.

Chapter 33

With my forehead pressed against the cold window, I watched one rolling, sepia hill after another pass beneath the wing of the plane. Above the horizon, the deep blue of the cloudless sky was a sharp contrast. We were three weeks into the new century, and the beginning of the fifth year of my No Pudge! journey. The plane banked to the left, and the abrupt change from drab sameness to lush green made me catch my breath.

"Welcome to Palm Springs." These were the first words my silver-haired seatmate had uttered since planting her tan, slender self in the seat next to mine. "Is this your first time here?"

"It is." I turned back to look out the window.

The plane was starting its descent towards the airport, gliding over green-velvet golf courses and large homes with Caribbean-blue swimming pools.

"Are you here to play golf?"

I tore my eyes away from the scene below. "No, I'm here for a trade show." *Actually, I'm here to jump off a cliff.*

I was about to attend the National Food Distributors Association Show, a no-frills show for distributors and food companies only. No elaborate, oversized booths, no wasted time talking to people who couldn't really impact your business. The first day of the show was spent in ten-minute, face-to-face meetings with potential distributors. The second day, the distributors walked the show floor visiting booths of companies that had caught their interest, nailing down agreements, and, in many cases, placing orders.

I was about to have an encounter of the mega kind with a bunch of the Big Boys and I was nervous. I would have been totally freaked out if I'd known what was coming.

Lugging a leaning tower of cases through a labyrinth of hotel hallways, I searched for what I assumed would be a small meeting room. My arms were aching, and I was getting a crick in my neck by the time I finally found the doorway and walked through. *Holy shit.* My small meeting room was the hotel ballroom, and it was completely filled with people and rows of rectangular tables. Each table had two chairs on each side and a tall stand in the center with the name of a distributor; the tables were arranged alphabetically by distributor name. The distributor reps were all seated at their tables facing the door, waiting for the meetings to begin.

I joined the throngs (yes, *throngs*) of people standing along the inside wall. Most were relaxed and chatting comfortably, but a few were standing by themselves with an "I don't feel so good" look on their faces. I knew exactly how they felt.

Looking around, trying to locate the table of my first appointment, I suddenly realized I was looking at a sea of male faces. Every one of the waiting distributor reps was a man. Not one female face, friendly or un-, among them. *Crap, this must be what "speed dating" is like.*

A bell sounded. With schedules and samples and sell sheets in hand, the crowd moved as fast as politely possible to their first appointments. People started talking even before their butts landed in the chairs, afraid to lose even a few seconds of their precious ten-minute face time.

I dropped my armload on the table of my first appointment and extended my hand to the thin, balding man opposite me. "Hi, I'm Lindsay Frucci from No Pudge!."

He was leaning back, his chair balanced on two legs, arms folded across his royal-blue polo-shirted chest. Rather than reach for my hand, he dropped forward and looked down at a paper on the table in front of him. "Nope," he shook his head. "You're not on our list. Must be the next table."

"Sorry," I mumbled as I loaded my things back into my arms and turned towards the next table, running headlong into two men in suits standing right behind me.

"We're supposed to be here." They sidled by me and quickly sat down. Out of the corner of my eye, I saw Bald Guy reach across the table for a hearty handshake.

Feeling like a salmon swimming upstream, I fought my way to the next table. A very round man with neatly parted dark hair and a trim mustache hefted himself upright. "You must be Lindsay," he said as he reached toward the stack in my arms. "Let me help you with that." Beside him, a ruddy-faced guy smiled warmly and gestured towards one of the waiting chairs. "Take a seat. We've been waiting for you."

Phew. Right table. Better table.

After settling in the chair, I launched into my speech. Although they were attentive, when they learned of my sparse, New England–only distribution, their enthusiasm waned. Almost as an afterthought I mentioned Weight Watchers. Both men snapped to attention. *Hmmm. . .* I told them about our Leader Sampling Program (making it sound, of course, much bigger than it was). Their eyes sparkled, and they practically drooled. Strobe lights flashed in my brain, bells clanged. *Think I've stumbled onto something.*

In no time, I was starting off each session with the tidbit about our sampling program. As I moved through the room, I left a swath of excited men in my wake. I felt like a long-legged blonde with big boobs.

That day I learned just how powerful the Weight Watchers consumer is. She has a reputation for searching out and actually buying a product she's read or heard about. If she can't find it, she asks for it. I was still a tiny unknown, but the magic "WW" gave me instant credibility and pushed the door open another inch or two.

These crazy, chaotic two days saved me and others like me from flying all over the country to call on each distributor individually. Even if I could've afforded all those plane tickets, 99 percent of those guys wouldn't have given me the time of day. This show let me get a foot in the Big Boys' door, and I walked away with serious interest from several distributors covering "No Pudge!–less" parts of the country. The next step was to get the mixes out of these distributors' warehouses and into grocery stores where real live people shopped. And this step was gonna be a killer.

The money-eating Slotting Monster was alive and thriving and had an insatiable appetite. And it didn't give a flying fig about lines drawn in the sand.

Chapter 34

Paul is Italian. I mean *Italian.* His parents were both from the "old country" and his mother, Josephina, lived for ninety-four years believing that life revolved around three things: the Catholic Church, Family, and Food. Not necessarily in that order.

His earliest memory is waking up on Sunday morning to the smell of garlic sizzling in olive oil as his mother made the sauce for Sunday dinner. Their tiny, three-bedroom ranch had two kitchens (one in the basement). Dinner was the main event of the day and something his mother started planning well in advance.

I, on the other hand, was raised by a Yankee woman who hated to cook and believed that if God had wanted us to cook with fresh ingredients, He wouldn't have created frozen and canned. I learned to love cooking as an adult and was happy to plan and prepare dinner — just not every night. Especially when I'd spent the entire day in my office, trying to push a huge freaking boulder up a steep freaking hill. Through a mine field.

One day, Paul walked through my office on his way to the kitchen for lunch (*lunch? Who takes time for lunch?*). "What're we havin' for dinner?" he asked.

"Whatever you want to make." I said without looking up. It was meant as a joke. Sorta.

He paused for the briefest moment before continuing to the kitchen. A little while later, he walked back through. "I took some chicken out of the freezer."

Huh?

At around four o'clock he came out of his office and headed back downstairs — this time without a word. I heard him banging around in the kitchen.

A car pulled in the driveway, followed closely by another. Both dogs snapped to attention. Before car doors could slam shut, two furry, four-legged rockets were racing each other down the stairs. From my desk I heard the back door open and a melody of happily whimpering dogs blended with the "Hi baby" cooing of adolescent boys.

My office was suddenly filled with a cloud of testosterone as six lanky teenaged boys tromped up the stairs. "Hi, Mom!" "Hey, Mrs. Frucci!" The daily routine was a quick stop to say hi to me and then off to the kitchen. Adam glanced at Paul's open door. "Where's Dad?"

"In the kitchen." I lowered my voice to a conspiratorial whisper, "I think he's making dinner!"

The cloud moved to the stairs and stampeded down.

"Hey, Old Man," I heard Adam say. "Whatcha doin'?"

"Making dinner." Paul's reply was music to my ears. "Someone has to."

I grinned. *Can't argue with that. Might as well be you.*

The Universe was starting to tilt in a direction I liked. I was going to stay in my office and not do or say anything that might put it back on its previous axis.

Ask my kids today who made dinner most nights while they were in high school and they'd say, "Dad." He discovered that he loved the creativity of cooking and I discovered that I loved not having to think about it.

Although the "what to have for dinner" worry was now off my plate (pardon the pun), I was still totally overwhelmed. As soon as I got the kids out the door in the morning, I cleaned the kitchen, put in a load of laundry, and went up to the office, where I veered from Grand Poohbah to sales manager to CFO to PR person to pack-and-ship girl. My day ended at around ten p.m., when Paul came to the bottom of the stairs, announced "You're done," and turned off the light.

Late one night, I was hunched over my desk, staring at the glow of my computer screen, when I realized that A.J. was standing quietly in the doorway, watching me. "You know what, Mom?"

"What?" I didn't look up.

"You're a slave to the Pig."

I turned around. "Excuse me?"

"You heard me."

He turned and walked out.

Shit.

There was no doubt I was working long hours, but No Pudge! was growing. Just not fast enough. I wanted to be taking *bigger* steps.

Then in March, the new publisher of *Weight Watchers* magazine called to ask if I might be interested in placing an ad. In return, she'd print another mention of the brownie mixes. I jumped in with both feet and committed to ads in the next six issues.

Shortly after the first ad came out, I got a frantic call.

"I'm Mike, the grocery manager for the Hy-Vee store in Grand Island, Nebraska. You gotta help me."

Nebraska? "I'll do my best. What do you need?"

"I need some No Pudge! — and fast! They have these Weight Watchers meetings next door? Soon as the last meeting was over, five ladies marched in here and told me I had to get some. I don't even know what it is, but I'm afraid of what they might do to me if I don't get it. Soon."

I love it I love it I love it! "Bless their little hearts!"

"Believe me, there was nothing little about any of these ladies."

I went back to work, grinning like a fool. This was undeniable proof that the time and expense of sending out all those sample packs to Weight Watchers leaders was starting to have an impact. Hy-Vee was a 200-store chain that covered seven Midwestern states. Eighteen months later, No Pudge! would be on the shelf in every store. Our growing popularity among Weight Watchers members, combined with reviews in *Kiplinger's, Self, Chocolatier,* and *Entrepreneur,* as well as several major newspapers, was pushing the business forward.

But as the business grew, so did hassles with packaging. The bags tore and got squashed, and neither distributors nor grocery stores liked dealing with them. It was time to make the big leap to boxes.

Why hadn't I gone with boxes to begin with? Because I assumed that a printed box with an inner bag would be far more expensive than a printed bag. It wasn't. Should I have checked into it before automatically going with bags? Ya think?

Working with Peter on size and Lee on design, we kept the colors and basic design from the bags, but had fun tweaking and improving. Tall and slim, the new boxes didn't take up any more shelf space than our bags and were different from every other brownie mix box out there.

The unanimously positive reaction from my distributors reinforced my decision. I hadn't realized the bags had screamed "small company" and "temporary" to distributors and grocers. Now my skinny, smiling pig smiled confidently from a solid, well-sealed box that quietly said "real company" and "here to stay."

Chapter 35

"I can't do this anymore." I was sitting on the edge of the bed, my face buried in my hands.

Paul stuck his head around the bathroom door. "Whacha say?"

"I . . . can't . . . do this . . . anymore." I collapsed backwards on the bed. "I can't, I can't, I can't."

He didn't ask what I meant. This was my standard Sunday night rant. "Then don't," he said.

"Oh, thanks. That's really helpful."

He sighed and sat down on the bed next to me. "Honey, what do you want me to say?"

"I don't know," I moaned. "I'm just so overwhelmed. I want to quit, but I own the damn company!"

"Hang in there, babe," he said, patting my leg. "Vacation's coming."

"Not soon enough," I grumbled. "It's not tomorrow."

Three weeks later we headed to the Caribbean for a long-awaited family vacation. We had a great week of swimming and sunning, but when we checked out, the phone bill was $500. A No Pudge! crisis had erupted and I'd spent an hour on the phone every afternoon while my family splashed in the ocean. It wasn't exactly the break I'd been hoping for.

It was like I'd stepped into quicksand. If I didn't find some way to bring balance into my life soon, I'd be in danger of disappearing.

Then, I turned fifty.

My birthday is in early August, and we spent a glorious weekend at Paul's brother's house on Lake Winnipesaukee. We swam, boated, got too much sun, and laughed. As the sun was setting low over the lake, my sister-in-law handed me a glass of wine. "I've got the kitchen under control. Go sit somewhere and relax. You've earned it."

Settling into an Adirondack chair by the shore, I took a long sip of wine and gazed across a lake crowned with the beauty of a spectacular summer sunset. With each breath, I felt the serenity of my surroundings loosen the tightness in my shoulders and chest. I couldn't remember the last time I had slowed down enough to just "be."

A.J. was right. I was a slave to the pig. More than halfway through my life, I'd allowed myself to settle into a place where I was miserable. *It's time to take back control, girl.*

On the ride home, I turned to face my three guys. "I have an announcement to make."

"Uh oh," Adam muttered.

"I've decided to set some boundaries around work. From now on, I'm gonna stay out of the office after dinner and on weekends."

"About time." A.J. raised a hand for a high five.

I leaned over to slap it. "I'm not done. I'm also going to hire someone to help handle sales and manage the brokers."

"Awesome, Mom!"

"Good decision," Paul nodded. "It's time."

I wasn't sure how I was going to afford to hire someone of the caliber and experience I needed, but I knew I couldn't afford not to. Happy Birthday to me.

Two weeks after I sent the word out that I was looking for a National Sales Manager, a woman with solid experience in the natural-foods industry sent me her résumé. We had a short chat and agreed to meet for lunch the following Thursday, September 13, 2001.

On Tuesday morning, I was out early, anxious to get errands done before the workday started. A little after nine, I pulled back into the garage. Linda met me at the door. "Two planes hit the World Trade Center towers."

As her words sank in, I gave a silent prayer of thanks that I knew where my guys were. Paul was in Boston at a meeting, Adam was probably asleep in his dorm, and A.J. was safely in class at Brady.

When I walked in the door, the phone was ringing.

"Mom, did you hear what happened?" Adam had been a freshman at Syracuse University for less then two weeks.

"Yes sweetie. I just heard."

"Where's Dad?"

Like millions of Americans, I sat transfixed in front of our living-room television, watching in horror as the towers fell and rescue workers desperately searched for loved ones amid the smoking rubble.

If turning fifty had made me realize life was short, the heartbreaking and terrifying events of September 11 confirmed it. I called the woman I was scheduled to interview and postponed our lunch. I wanted to stay close to home.

One week later on another perfect, blue-sky day, I walked into Legal Seafood looking for someone I'd never met, who looked like she was looking for someone she had never met.

"Lindsay?"

I turned to face a conservatively dressed, petite woman with sparkling green eyes and a radiant smile. Her thick, wavy auburn hair was cut short and brushed back from her face.

"Sallie?" When I stuck out my hand, she grasped it firmly.

We spent the next hour and a half talking about everything from the Twin Towers to No Pudge! to kids. Before the waitress brought the bill, I offered her the job. By the time it was paid, she'd accepted.

A few weeks before, I'd been in an exhausted, blue, barely-keeping-my-head-above-water funk. Then Sallie showed up. Any number of people could have shown up to rescue me, but any number didn't. Sallie did. She didn't know that's what she was doing, but rescue me she did.

A quick study, she soon became a knowledgeable and enthusiastic No Pudge! ambassador. When she wasn't traveling, she worked from home, and for the next three and a half years, we talked on the phone almost every day. We worked hard and learned a lot from each other, but rarely lost sight of the fact that it was important to have fun while doing it. For example, she learned how to deal with specialty-food brokers and distributors, and I learned how to drink "big-girl drinks."

During one of our first trade shows together, we spent an afternoon wandering Chicago's Miracle Mile, the best window shopping west of Fifth Avenue in New York. In Pottery Barn, I picked up a martini glass. "I wish I liked martinis," I sighed. "People who drink them always look so sophisticated."

Sallie stopped mid-stride and turned back. "You do know that you don't have to drink martinis to have a drink in a martini glass." She arched one eyebrow. "Right?"

Feeling like a total hick, I shook my head.

"Lots of good drinks are served in a martini glass. We'll try one at dinner tonight." She tucked her arm through mine. "Stick with me, I'll teach you how to drink like a big girl."

That night, settled at the bar in a cozy neighborhood restaurant in Chicago's Little Italy, Sallie ordered me a cosmo and herself a vodka gimlet straight up with a twist. When they arrived, I held my glass gently between my thumb and forefinger, desperately trying not to spill any of the delicate pink liquid that came right to the rim.

"Here's to your first big-girl drink!" she said with a grin.

We gently clinked glasses.

"The first of many!" Cautiously, I raised the glass to my lips and took a sip. *So this is what having fun feels like. . . .*

One of my primary goals back in 1999 had been to make contact with the buyers from Food Emporium, a high-end grocery chain with stores all over New York City. If you wanted a presence in NYC, you wanted Food Emporium.

So I'd wormed my way into the Haddon House Distributor Show that May and, on the first night, mustered up the courage to ask the rep for Food Emporium if he would bring their buyer by my booth. I'm tall, but as he looked down his nose at me, I felt myself shrinking. He coolly informed me my mixes were not a Food Emporium item and would never sell in New York. Although I was afraid he might be right, I told him he was wrong. With absolute conviction, he assured me he was not.

By 2002, thanks to loyal consumers requesting the mix, No Pudge! was in every Food Emporium in New York City. At the Haddon House show that spring, Sallie and I were standing in our booth when I turned to see that same Food Emporium rep striding purposefully down the aisle in our direction. Three or four men in suits trailed behind him. This was the first time I'd seen him since our unpleasant encounter three years earlier.

Everyone wanted these guys to stop at his or her booth, so their journey down the aisle was closely watched. They moved quickly, coming to a halt only when they were standing directly in front of us. The rep looked at me with a broad smile. “Lindsay, I’d like to introduce you to the buyers from Food Emporium.”

I smiled and shook hands with each one.

“The mixes are doing great,” he continued. “Everyone is thrilled.”

“That’s wonderful,” I said. “Obviously, we’re thrilled too!”

Then his smile faded, his eyes grew serious.

Uh oh. Here comes the “but. . .”

“I owe you an apology,” he said.

Say what?

“I was wrong about you and No Pudge!. I thought you were just another nice lady with a nice little product. I didn’t think you’d make it. But you’re still here and you’ve done a great job. I’m impressed. So are a lot of other people.” The group of men behind him beamed and nodded.

Whoa. “Thank you, Steve,” I finally managed. “That means a lot.”

With a wave, he and his group were off down the aisle. I stared at their retreating backs. Finally Sallie shook my arm. “You can pick your chin up off the floor now.”

I told her the whole story and her eyes widened. “He came to *apologize*? Wow. Bet that doesn’t happen often.”

The glow from that apology should have lasted for months. But then came the Summer from Hell.

Chapter 36

One afternoon in early June, I was working at my desk when Paul called. He'd left before breakfast for a meeting in Boston, and I hadn't talked to him all day.

"Hey Babe," I answered. "On your way home?"

"Just left."

"Get your stitches out?" He'd had a lymph node in his neck that kept popping out every time he turned his head, and I'd finally talked him into having it removed. He'd stopped at the doctor's office to get the stitches out on his way to Boston.

"Uh huh."

He sounds kind of . . . flat. "How'd it go?"

"Fine."

Something's not right. "Really?"

"Uh huh."

I was now sitting up straight in my chair. "What's going on?"

"Nothing."

"Bullshit. What aren't you telling me?"

Silence.

Alarms started clanging in my brain. "Frooch, this is me. What's going on?" The pounding in my ears was so loud that, when he answered, I wasn't sure I heard him correctly.

"The lymph node was malignant."

What?

"The pathology report showed some kind of leukemia. They're setting up an appointment for me to see an oncologist."

This can't be right. I was suddenly sick to my stomach. The surgeon had told him it looked completely normal. I closed my eyes. *I've clearly stumbled into someone else's life.*

It occurred to me he'd been carrying this devastating news around with him all day, tucked away in a little box, hoping if he kept the lid on tight enough, maybe it would just go away. A chill crept up my spine.

"Honey," I said softly, "when were you going to tell me?"

"Don't know. Hadn't gotten that far."

The word "malignant" kept ricocheting around my brain, making it hard to breathe. I forced air deep into my lungs, and as I slowly exhaled, the coping mechanism I'd acquired in my years as an emergency-room nurse kicked in. A sense of calm slipped over me. Right now, the priority was getting him home safely. "Listen, babe," I said. "Whatever this is, we'll deal with it. Together. Just come home, and we'll talk when you get here."

After I hung up the phone, I sat motionless, waiting for the room to stop spinning. Then I lowered my face to my hands and sobbed.

When he got home, we closed ourselves in our bedroom and I made him tell me everything. Apparently the doctor had not even read the pathology report before Paul arrived for his appointment. He'd walked into the room where Paul was waiting, read the report, turned white, and then fumbled around, reassuring Paul he was going to be fine. Paul had heard what he needed to hear — that he was going to be fine — and repeated that to me.

He'd been raised to believe that doctors were infallible super-beings whose judgment was not to be questioned. Because of my nursing background, I knew that doctors were smart people who sometimes made stupid mistakes. I also knew that every patient needed to be his own advocate and that the polite but seriously squeaky wheel got the most attention. We never discussed it, but both of us understood from that moment on I would take control.

We'd agreed not to say anything to the kids until we knew more, so Friday morning I perched on the edge of our bed to call the surgeon's office. With Linda in the office, A.J. studying for finals, and Adam home from college, it was the only private spot in the house. When the receptionist answered, I asked her if they'd made an appointment for Paul with the oncologist.

"Yes, Mrs. Frucci. The first opening is August 6th."

Are you fucking kidding me? "August 6th?!"

"Yes," she replied, as if this were nothing out of the ordinary. "It's a very busy practice and they need extra time for a new patient."

My first inclination was to climb through the phone and rip her head off, but instead I took a deep breath and kept my voice icily calm. "That is two months from now."

"I realize that, but. . ."

"I am sure," I continued as if she hadn't said a word, "you find that as unacceptable as I do. On three separate occasions over the past year, Dr. Locke told my husband that his enlarged node did not need to be removed and was nothing to worry about. Now we find out it's malignant." I paused to let that sink in. "We need to know if that delay has had a negative impact."

There was a brief moment of silence, then: "Absolutely. I'll call them back and let them know we need something sooner."

Less than five minutes later she called back. "Mrs. Frucci? I spoke to the nurse at the oncologist's office, and Dr. Briletti will see Paul next Tuesday at eleven."

At 11:10 a.m. the following Tuesday we were ushered into Dr. Briletti's office. I disliked him almost immediately. A generic-looking man with thinning dark hair and a lab coat so stiff that it rustled when he walked, he did his best to patently ignore me. Every time I asked a question, he would either dismiss it or direct his answer to Paul only.

After a quick exam, he flipped through Paul's chart, then crossed his arms over his starched white chest and regarded us across the room. "You have chronic lymphocytic leukemia," he said in a matter-of-fact tone. "More commonly known as CLL." Pause. "There's nothing we can do now. Once you start to have symptoms we can begin a standard chemotherapy regimen, but there's no cure." Another pause, then the *coup de grace.* "You probably have about five years. There's no rush, but I'd suggest you get your affairs in order."

My body turned to ice. I was afraid to reach for Paul's hand, fearful that human touch would break the semblance of control I was desperately trying to hold onto. Briletti rambled on about setting up a chest x-ray ("No rush") and an appointment to see him again in six months. We were being dismissed. I couldn't seem to move my body, but my brain continued to whir, desperately searching for questions I should be asking.

"Bone marrow transplant?" I finally came up with.

"Too old."

"Bone marrow biopsy?"

"Maybe later." Then, with a smile: "This is good news. I tell people all the time they only have five months! Five years is a gift."

Paul had turned fifty-two three days before.

Numb, we walked to the car in silence. Still not touching.

Paul put the key in the ignition, but rather than turning it, he sat with his hands resting on the steering wheel, staring straight ahead. I watched his pale profile and fought the nausea and hysteria rising in my throat. I was terrified to open my mouth, unsure of what would come crashing out. He closed his eyes briefly then turned to me. His face was expressionless, but in those dark brown eyes I could see fear and disbelief. "Want to go get lunch somewhere?"

I nodded.

Lunch? Yes. It was noon, so it was lunchtime. Normal. Familiar. Safe.

Fifteen minutes later we were seated at a concrete picnic table tucked in a corner of a strip-mall parking lot, next to a busy intersection. I was only vaguely aware of cars whizzing around us. Sandwiches, chips, and drinks that I barely remembered buying sat untouched on the table.

Our conversation was limited. It was impossible to put words to the tornado of emotions we were both feeling. I said we needed to find another doctor, and he didn't disagree. He said he didn't want to tell anyone, and I said we had to tell the boys. I would do it. He agreed.

We sat in the blazing sun in a dusty parking lot and let the fact that we had just been told he had five years to live sink in.

When we finally arrived home, both boys were out. Paul disappeared into his office and closed the door. I wasn't ready to make idle chitchat with Linda in the office, and I sure as hell wasn't in the mood for No Pudge! anything, so I headed for the kitchen. We knew a doctor at the Dartmouth-Hitchcock Medical Center in Lebanon, New Hampshire. I found her number, had her paged, and told her what Briletti had told us.

"That's outrageous!" She was furious. "Let me make a couple of calls and I'll call you right back."

Two days later we sat in another oncologist's office waiting for another opinion. I knew we were in the right place when the doctor walked in, introduced herself with a warm handshake for both of us, and spent an hour taking a history, doing a careful exam, and patiently answering every question we had.

Leaning towards Paul, she touched his knee and looked into his eyes. "You are too young for this. I can't tell you whether you have five years or twenty-five years, but I can promise you, we'll fight this with everything we have." I reached over and took Paul's hand. "There's every reason to feel hopeful," she said.

Over the next few weeks Paul worked on accepting his diagnosis and I worked on learning everything I could about it. Both boys seemed to handle their dad's diagnosis pretty well. The fact that Paul didn't look or feel "sick" made it easier for all of us to push the "c-word" into the background. Easier for the boys, that is — though not as easy, I'm sure, for Paul.

During my years of owning No Pudge!, I'd filled dozens of spiral notebooks with day-to-day notes. They are the journals of a business — factual and unemotional. But when I look back at June and July of 2002, oncologists' names, hospital phone numbers, and the internet addresses of cancer websites punctuate routine to-do lists and phone messages.

Flipping through those pages years later, I found myself rubbing my tightly folded arms, trying to ward off a sudden chill. Memories of the fear that overshadowed our fragile optimism and my determined "business as usual" demeanor felt all too real. I know now, that that summer signaled the beginning of the end.

Chapter 37

Keeping my eyes on the highway, I reached for my travel mug and took a careful swallow of the warm tea, hoping it would calm my unsettled stomach. I had a busy day ahead of me and didn't want to worry that any minute I might lose my cookies on my open-toed pumps.

Other than my mild case of the queasies, it was a gorgeous August morning, the traffic was light, and the car was sun-filled and blissfully quiet. I was whizzing towards Massachusetts to join Sallie for a meeting with our New England brokers. After the meeting we had plans to hit a nearby mall for some "girlfriend time."

I felt calm and at peace. Paul was feeling good and life in the Frucci household had settled back into a comfortable summer routine. Once again, my focus was zeroed in on pushing the "Pig" onward and upward.

Frank and Art were already seated in the conference room when Sallie and I walked in. We settled ourselves across the table from them and were exchanging pleasantries when I became aware of what felt like the fluttering of butterfly wings in my chest. I couldn't remember feeling anything like it before. Taking a slow, deep breath, I hoped to stop whatever was going on. The fluttering continued. Suddenly, Sallie's voice seemed to be coming from a great distance. I remember thinking that I'd better tell someone I was going to faint, just before the world went black.

When I opened my eyes, Art's arms were around my waist, keeping me from falling out of my chair, and my head was hanging between my knees. I started to raise my head to reassure everyone I was fine, but immediately the room started to fade. *Whoa.*

"Don't move. Keep your head down." Sallie's voice was close. My hands and feet were icy cold and felt like they were vibrating. When I raised my hands to look at them, they were the color of marble.

"Lindsay, please stay still." Art's voice was strained.

"I called 911," Frank said from across the room. "The paramedics are on their way."

Oh God. "I'm fine. I just fainted."

"They're already on their way." Sallie said. "And you are not fine."

Out of the corner of my eye, I saw three men in blue uniforms come bursting into the room. I tried to raise my head to convince them I was fine, but once again, the room began to fade to black.

Two men lowered me to the floor. "How ya doin'?" one asked as he wrapped a blood-pressure cuff around my arm. He looked up at the anxious faces around him. "The EMTs are on their way. We're the fire department."

"Please, oh please, don't tell me you came in a fire truck," I implored the cute fireman hovering above me.

"Big red one," he grinned. "Sirens and all."

Two more men dashed in, hauling a stretcher, and my fireman was replaced by an EMT. "I'm feeling better," I told him, "but my hands and feet are tingling."

"That's 'cause your blood pressure's so low. We're gonna take you to the hospital and get you checked out."

"I'll call Paul," Sallie said.

"No! He has enough on his plate without freaking out over nothing. I'll call him later." I figured I'd get checked out and be home before supper.

But by the time we arrived at the hospital, I was coming to grips with the fact that I hadn't "just fainted." It had been an hour since I'd blacked out, and I still felt incredibly weak.

In the Emergency Room I told the doctors I was a former ER nurse, believing that fact would give me credibility. They still asked the same questions over and over. "Was this a stressful meeting?" "Was the room really warm?" "Are you under a lot of stress at home?" Knowing what a teaching hospital is like, I tried to be patient, but finally I'd had enough. "Stop patronizing me," I snarled at what felt like the fiftieth young doctor to ask those questions. "I am not an hysterical female, and this was not an anxiety attack."

It was a medical student who finally asked if I'd noticed any change in my stamina. When I thought about it, I realized I had been short of breath recently during workouts. I'd figured it just meant I wasn't pushing myself hard enough. No one mentioned it again, but that moment stands out in my mind as the first time I began to worry that something might really be wrong. The fact no one else had thought to ask that question, or to follow up on the answer, is a strong indication that the diagnosis of "hysterical female" had already been determined.

For three more hours they continued to question, poke, prod, x-ray, and stick me with needles, and there was still no indication that I was about to be released. It was clear I wasn't going to be home by supper. I called Paul and told him I'd fainted, assuring him I was fine but probably shouldn't drive home. Could he come down with Adam to pick me up?

After I hung up, the doctor in charge of the ER came in, pulled up a stool, and sat next to the stretcher. "If you weren't an ER nurse I'd probably put this down as fainting and send you home, especially since you were only out for a few seconds."

"She wasn't out for a few seconds." They'd finally let Sallie come in from the waiting room, and she was sitting beside me. "She was out for a good minute or more."

He raised his eyebrows. "Really?"

If you hadn't left her sitting in the damn waiting room for three hours, maybe she could've told you earlier.

He turned back to me. "Well, that makes me feel better about my decision. I'm admitting you for the night."

Just before they came to take me to my room, Paul arrived with Adam. I assured them I felt *fine* (Sallie announced that this word was getting obnoxiously repetitious) but they were keeping me overnight as a precaution. Sallie drove Adam to my car and both headed home. I was sure the first thing she would do when she walked in the door was pour a big glass of wine. It was what I wanted to do.

Paul headed out to pick up a few necessities for me, including a book to keep me occupied and some supper for both of us. I was admitted to a general medical floor, attached to a monitor, and left alone.

The next morning a technician arrived to do an echocardiogram, an ultrasound that would show how efficiently my heart was pumping. After lunch, a crowd of white coats descended on the room. In the lead was the cardiologist, a tall, handsome man with thick black hair and glasses that sat on the tip of his nose. A couple of residents, an intern, a group of medical students, and the charge nurse followed dutifully in his wake, congregating at the foot of the bed. In a slightly clipped, Indian accent, the cardiologist told me the monitor hadn't picked up any irregularities in my heart rate or rhythm, and his assumption was that I'd fainted. His office would arrange a six-month follow-up, and I should call him if anything else happened. I was free to go.

After they left, I called Paul, got dressed, and had just settled into a chair with my book when the cardiologist and his entire entourage came sweeping back into the room. If you'd worked in a teaching hospital for as long as I had, you'd know that when a busy staff doctor comes back to your room after you've been discharged but before you've managed to make your escape, you are screwed.

The cardiologist sat down on the bed. The rest of the crowd stood politely at a distance.

Uh oh.

"Mrs. Frucci," he said quietly. "I'm afraid I have very bad news. We've just looked at your echo. Your heart is quite enlarged and is not working efficiently." He paused to let that sink in.

I stared at him. All I could think of was Paul. *How am I going to tell Frooch? This is the last thing he needs.* I finally managed to find my voice. "What do you think is going on?"

"We honestly aren't sure. It could be a virus has settled in your heart, but you haven't had any viral symptoms. What we do know is that you can't go home. I'm going to schedule you for an arteriogram in the morning and then we'll do a study to see how irritable your heart is. Yesterday's episode may have been ventricular fibrillation. We may need to put in a defibrillator."

V-fib? Defibrillator?

"I know this is a lot to take in all at once. Is your husband on his way?"

"He should be here shortly. But this is going to be hard for him." My throat tightened. I could feel the burn of impending tears. "He was diagnosed with leukemia in June."

"I'm very sorry." He stood. Teary female — he was out of his element. "I'm going to do some charting. If I'm not at the desk when your husband arrives, have one of the nurses page me, and I will come right back to talk with him."

If you're screwed when the busy doctor comes back to your room after discharging you, you are doubly screwed if he offers to come right back again as soon as your husband arrives.

The entourage followed him out. A young nurse helped me undress, put me back in bed, and hooked up the monitor.

When Paul arrived, the cardiologist explained what was going on. He said he'd have more information after the tests were done. When he left, we sat together quietly — each trying hard to be brave and strong for the other. I'm sure Paul's ride home that night was long and lonely.

I remember waiting on the stretcher outside the arteriogram room the next morning, working hard to hold back tears, and then bantering with the doctor while watching the dye flow through my arteries on the monitor. The cardiologist showed up to watch.

"Her arteries aren't just clear, they're pristine," the arteriogram doctor announced. That sounded like good news, but I didn't get the sense anyone was celebrating. A blocked artery would have been a simple explanation, leading to a straightforward fix.

When I got back to my room, the cardiologist's physician's assistant came in to show me what a defibrillator looked like. A thin, silver-colored disk, about three inches in circumference, it looked huge.

No way you're putting that thing in me. That's for old people!

As she was explaining my next procedure, two women in scrubs arrived. They wheeled me through the halls and into what looked like an operating room with a bunch of computer equipment lining one wall. The cardiologist, barely recognizable in full surgical garb, explained he was going to thread a catheter with an electrode from my femoral artery into my heart, then stimulate my heart to see if he could reproduce what had happened the day before. I'd get a mild sedative through the IV, but would be awake.

Once the catheter was in place, he walked to the bank of computers and announced that I would feel my heart rate increase slightly. Almost immediately, I felt the same fluttering in my chest. "That's it. That's what I felt," I remember saying before the room went dark. When I woke up, all was the same — no one was hurrying, no one seemed worried. But my chest felt strange, and my stomach was churning.

"I'm going to do that again, Lindsay," he said from across the room. "You okay?"

Oh yeah, I'm just fuckin' ducky. You? "I don't like that feeling. Are you almost done?"

"Just one more time. Here we go." Again, the fluttering. Again, a slip into nothingness. Then a calm voice penetrated the darkness. "She has no palpable blood pressure." I remember thinking, *I'm here, I'm still here,* before descending back into blackness. My next conscious thought was that it hurt to breathe. "My chest hurts."

"I know," came a female voice from above me. "That's because we had to shock you."

"Lindsay?" a deep voice said.

I opened my eyes. A pair of dark brown eyes floated close above me, sandwiched between a surgical cap and mask. The eyes were attached to the deep voice I recognized as my cardiologist. "Your heart went into ventricular fibrillation very easily. We had to shock it back to normal rhythm. We need to put in a defibrillator."

I closed my eyes. "No." I was groggy, my chest hurt, and I felt like I was going to throw up. I just wanted to go back to my room and be left alone. "Maybe tomorrow. . ."

"We can't wait until tomorrow," the voice said. "The anesthesiologist is here and he's going to put you to sleep."

This time when I woke up, I was on a stretcher in a hallway. Paul was close by talking with the cardiologist. I couldn't make out what they were saying. Behind him stood my niece, Kim — my New York Fancy Food Show compatriot.

I managed a groggy, "Hey."

Immediately Paul was leaning over the stretcher holding my hand. "Hey, babe. How you doing?"

"Fine." Auto-response. "Chest hurts."

"The doctor had to put in a defibrillator."

"'Kay." And I drifted off. I never asked Paul what the doctor said to him in the corridor that afternoon, but I know that it scared the hell out of him. I didn't want to know how potentially lethal the prognosis was. I just wanted to get home and get better.

Before I was discharged, the physician's assistant tried to warn me that my new internal insurance policy (my defibrillator), would likely go off soon and often.

"It's never going off," I told her.

"Well, I hope you're right," she said patiently, "but your heart is very irritable. The chances that you'll have another episode are extremely high."

"Yeah, well, it's not going off," I repeated. Unrealistically stubborn? Uh huh. Scared to death and in total denial? Oh, you betcha. I flatly refused to accept that the little appliance in my chest was going to go off and leave me feeling like I'd been kicked in the chest by a horse. And it hasn't. As of this writing — eight years and counting — it has never gone off.

Two days later I was discharged with a big bandage over my upper left chest and a pharmacy of pills. Our boys had handled their father's diagnosis very well, primarily because he didn't look or act sick. I, on the other hand, looked awful. The cardiac drugs lowered my blood pressure and left me tired, pale, and short of breath. When I walked in the door, the expressions on the kids' faces hit me hard.

Refusing to "go upstairs and lie down," I settled in the kitchen. Sue had come over and was making me a cup of tea. A.J. hopped up to sit on the counter while Adam foraged in the refrigerator and Paul washed dishes.

"Are you going back to Lahey, or are you going to try to find a cardiologist closer?" Sue asked as she put the kettle back on the stove.

"Lahey." I reached out and wrapped my hands around the warm cup she handed me. "Hey, it's right next door to the Burlington Mall. My appointments will be the perfect excuse to go shopping!"

Adam stuck his head around the refrigerator door. "Leave it to Mom to figure that out."

"Yeah," my husband retorted. "Your mother would die if she couldn't shop!"

Everyone in the kitchen froze and seemed to hold their breath. I started to laugh. "You're absolutely right! There are priorities!"

There was an almost-audible collective sigh of relief.

On Paul and Sallie's strict orders I was forbidden to set foot in the office for at least a week. In my business journal from that period there are no entries between August 13 and August 18, so I guess I actually did as I was told. One week after I was allowed to return to work, Paul and Adam loaded up the SUV and once again we made the journey to Syracuse. We dropped Adam off in now-familiar surroundings and left him there, happy to start his sophomore year. A few days later A.J. began his senior year at Brady. The Summer from Hell was officially over.

Chapter 38

With both boys settled back into their respective school routines, Paul and I decided that a long weekend away was in order. Exploring the Maine coast would be a great way to put the insanity of the summer where it belonged — in the past — and to celebrate moving forward.

It was late September; the summer residents were gone and a quiet had settled over the area. For two days, we walked hand in hand along empty beaches, climbed sea-swept rocks, and explored narrow, winding roads that led to coastal villages.

Both chilly nights found us at a lobster pound in the tiny harbor of Five Islands. Bundled in fleece jackets, we sat outside at picnic tables eating steamers just plucked from the sea and drinking wine from paper cups. Shoveling lobster into our mouths with butter-sticky fingers, we agreed this trip had been just what the doctor ordered. After dinner, we settled in rocking chairs on the porch of our charming bed-and-breakfast and watched the moon rise over the water.

In the B-and-B living room I discovered a ferry schedule for Monhegan Island. My dad had been there to paint years before and had often talked about its rugged beauty. A day trip seemed like the perfect end to our mini-vacation.

Before leaving the charming harbor of Port Clyde the next morning, the captain of the ferry warned his passengers that the hour-long trip across the ten miles of ocean between Port Clyde and Monhegan would be rough. Anyone who wanted to change his mind was welcome to a full refund. Paul and I confidently assured each other we'd be fine. We never got seasick.

Ten minutes later, on the top deck of the ferry, it was only sheer force of will that kept us from throwing up all over each other. *Whose bright idea was this anyway? Oh yeah . . . mine.*

When the ferry finally docked at the island, we managed to stumble down the gangplank and stagger over to two Adirondack chairs perched nearby. Without a word, we collapsed into them. Leaning back, we waited for the earth to stop rocking beneath our feet.

Paul was the first to speak. "That was awful."

Without moving or opening my eyes I whispered, "Ya think?" and emitted a low groan. "And we have to do it all again in a few hours."

"Maybe the seas will be calmer by then."

"From your lips to God's ears," I managed.

"Honey, open your eyes — this is gorgeous."

I cautiously opened my eyes. Spread before me I saw small, sea-weathered, gray buildings nestled along the rocky shore of the tiny harbor. Large and small sailboats and fishing boats of every color rocked gently at their moorings. Beyond them, the steel-gray ocean met the brilliant blue sky. I sat up a little straighter. "Wow." Turning slightly in my chair, I looked at the Island Inn towering above me.

Like a dowager queen overseeing her harbor, this vintage nineteenth-century grande dame was dressed in cedar shingles silvered by age and accessorized by crisp, freshly painted white trim. A broad white verandah stretched across the front like a heavy pearl choker, and a widow's walk crowned the roof. Our chairs sat on a lush, green lawn that sloped gently to the rocky harbor.

"Feeling better?" Paul asked.

I turned to my handsome husband and smiled. "Yeah. How 'bout you?"

"Much." He pushed himself out of his chair and reached out a hand. "Ready to explore?"

The day had gotten off to a rather shaky start, but the sun was shining, the steady breeze still held a tinge of summer's warmth, and we had four wonderful hours before we had to subject ourselves to our return trip. Holding hands, we set off.

There are few homes on the island and no cars. Instead of paved roads, a network of walking and hiking trails provide access to rocky cliffs, spectacular views, and piney woods. We chose a trail that hugged the jagged coastline before climbing slowly in elevation.

Taking our time, we stopped often to take in the sights and smells of this wild island.

An hour and a half after we left the sanctuary of the Adirondack chairs, we were standing on a cliff, gazing out at the sun-dappled ocean. My eyes filled with tears. I sent a silent prayer heavenward. *Thank you, God, for letting me be here to share this beautiful place with Paul. I don't know why you spared me, but I want you to know how incredibly grateful I am. Thank you.*

As we headed back towards the village, an older couple, moving slowly ahead of us on the trail, stepped aside to let us pass.

"Don't want to hold up you young folks," the gentleman kidded as we walked past.

"If they only knew," I whispered to Paul with a giggle. "They're probably healthier than we are!"

By the time the ferry left the island for our return trip to the mainland, the seas had calmed considerably. This time we sat on the top deck, appreciated the journey, and fantasized about the decadent dinner of lobster drowning in melted butter that awaited us on terra firma.

The next morning we checked out early and headed home to watch Sunday football with A.J. We felt rested, energized, and ready to move forward.

My grateful, enthusiastic, I-can-do-this attitude disappeared in an instant with a single phone call from Sallie. "What?! The day before Thanksgiving at noon? Is he nuts?" For close to a year we'd been trying to get an appointment with a major southeastern chain that was headquartered in Atlanta, and we'd finally scored one for the second week of November. It was important enough that Sallie and I were both going and had already booked our flights.

"I can't believe it either." She was obviously upset. "He called this morning out of the blue and announced he'd rescheduled us. When I reminded him it was the day before Thanksgiving, he got really snooty. Said if we didn't want the business badly enough to rearrange our schedules, we shouldn't bother to come at all."

"I have sixteen people here the next day for dinner. And you have a crowd at your house!"

"Linds, I'll go if you want me to."

"Like hell you will. Thanks for offering, but there's no way you're screwing up your Thanksgiving because this guy is being an asshole. Clearly, he just shows up on holidays, after his wife has done all the damn work."

"Let me give it one more try." Sallie was working hard at being the calm voice of reason. "I'll tell him we'll come any other day that works for him."

"It's worth a shot."

I hung up the phone and sat there, fuming. This guy was being a jerk just because he could. It was that simple. I was tired of the "God" complex some of these buyers had. They expected us lowly vendors to bend to their every whim. My tolerance for that behavior had never been great, but in the last few months it had reached a new low. A year earlier I might have actually gotten on a plane and made the trip, but not now.

I reached for the phone and dialed a friend who had sold his company a year earlier. The last time I'd seen him, we'd talked about the ups and downs of the sales process.

"Tim, I'm thinking it might be time to sell No Pudge!." I told him about the Thanksgiving appointment mess.

"I want you to call the guy I worked with," he said. "His name is Steve Mintz. He usually deals with much bigger companies than No Pudge!, but tell him I told you to call. He's smart, good at what he does, and a good friend of mine. At the very least, he might be able to give you some guidance."

"Guidance is exactly what I need."

I put down the phone, leaned back, and stared out the window. Was I really ready to hand No Pudge! over to someone else? Sallie had only been with me a year, and we were doing well. It didn't seem fair for me to walk away, but I was so tired of the constant struggle.

The ringing phone interrupted my thoughts.

"I just hung up with Bill and he was adamant," Sallie said. "Either the twenty-seventh or not at all."

"Unbelievable."

"That's not all, it gets better!" No more calm voice of reason. She was mad. "Actually, he did offer another time. He's available at two that day if we would prefer it to noon."

We commiserated for another five minutes about what a jerk this guy was. When Sallie hung up, I hit Line 2 and quickly dialed the number Tim had given me.

"Steve Mintz."

He listened quietly as I introduced myself and told him why I was calling. "Tim's right, you're a lot smaller than the companies I usually work with, *and* you probably can't afford me, but I'd be happy to help you figure out if selling makes sense. Can I ask you a few questions?"

For the next hour he asked questions about the business and my reasons for wanting to sell. By the time we were ready to hang up, I had a list of financial reports he wanted me to e-mail him.

"I'm not sure I'll tell you what you want to hear," he told me. "But I can promise I'll give you my honest opinion."

That night at dinner, I unloaded to Paul and A.J. about the abruptly changed Thanksgiving meeting. Except for an indignant "You're kidding?" from Paul and "What an idiot!" from A.J., both remained focused on moving forkfuls of pasta from bowl to mouth.

"I've decided to sell No Pudge!." Both forks stopped in mid-air and two sets of eyes focused on me.

"Do you think it's big enough to make a sale worthwhile?" Paul asked.

Before I could answer, A.J. leaned across the table for a fist bump. "Good for you, Mom! You're a slave to the Pig. Get rid of it!"

His father raised his eyebrows. "You don't want her to keep it so you can take it over some day?"

"No way." A.J. shook his head for emphasis. "It's the last thing I'd want to do. Just make sure you sell it for a lot," he grinned. "So you can buy me season tickets to the Red Sox and the Celtics."

The next two days were busy, and although I accomplished everything I was supposed to, thoughts of selling and what I'd do with millions of dollars and loads of free time bounced around in my head. *I'm gonna throw a huge party and invite everyone I know. I'll make it a whole weekend and pay for everything to thank everyone who's helped me. Then I'll take a long vacation! Yeah, a spa vacation. And I'll take Sallie. Paul can retire, we'll travel the world and build our dream house.* With all the money Steve was going to sell my company for, there was no limit to all the wonderful things I could do. Life was gonna be sweet. . . .

"You can't sell yet. The company's too small," Steve said when I called him late Friday afternoon.

Huh? The visions of big parties and spa vacations vanished. I slumped back in my chair and felt a big rock settle in the pit of my stomach.

"But I am very impressed by what you've accomplished," he said into the long silence. "You've kept your costs down, and where you have spent, you've made good choices."

I sat up a little straighter. I was nice to hear someone who clearly knew what he was talking about tell me I'd done a good job. The rock felt a little lighter.

"I understand why you're thinking about selling," he continued. "But you need to hold on for another couple of years. I'd like to see a big push to increase sales and see you increase your margins by cutting costs in a couple of critical places." He continued to talk, but my brain was stuck.

Another couple of years? *Are you kidding me?* Big push? Cut costs? *How? Where?!*

"Look," he said gently, "I'm not going to lie to you. It is what it is."

And it sucks.

"But I've got some ideas about moving forward, and I'd like to help."

You said I couldn't afford you, remember? "I appreciate your offer, but what would that cost?"

"I'm not going to charge you anything. Just don't tell anyone I'm doing this for you. I can't afford to give advice away all the time, but I like you and I'm impressed by what you've done and how you've done it. When the time comes to sell, we'll have another conversation. For now let's just worry about getting you there."

For the next eighteen months, every workday ended with a long phone call with Steve. We talked about everything from dogs, spouses, and the weather, to kids (mine), aging parents (his) and of course, No Pudge!. It would be four months before we would come face to face for the first time and by then, he'd become one of my closest friends.

With Steve doling out a daily dose of "Atta girl!" combined with small business wisdom, and Sallie handling most of the travel, the desperation I'd felt about pushing that big boulder slowly dissipated.

As I handed out glasses of sparkling cider to the crew of high-school seniors assembled in our living room to watch the ball drop in Times Square, I thought back to the same scene one year ago. If we'd known what was coming, the celebration would have been a lot more subdued. But, thankfully, we hadn't known. We had weathered the terrible storms and emerged — not exactly unscathed, but standing.

I took my place between Paul and A.J. as we counted down the last seconds of 2002.

"Three, two, one!" The living room erupted in cheering.

Paul enveloped me in a hug. "Happy New Year, babe," he whispered in my ear.

"Happy New Year." I pulled back and held up my glass. "Here's to 2003 being a little less bumpy and a lot more boring."

He grinned and tapped my glass with his. "I'll drink to that!"

Chapter 39

As I moved forward into the new year, every financial decision I faced for No Pudge! had to answer the question — Will this help grow the business? I no longer fantasized about freedom or financial security. That kind of thinking would only distract me from my primary task for the next twelve months: increasing sales.

Sallie's heavy travel schedule, combined with my careful spending, was paying off. Sales were growing steadily. No Pudge! wasn't a household name yet, but within circles like Weight Watchers the brand was becoming known. I was ecstatic when I called Steve to tell him we'd finished the first quarter ahead of projections.

"That's great," he said. "But it only confirms to me that you shouldn't be thinking about selling."

"Why not?" I wasn't sure I wanted to hear his answer.

"Because you're on the cusp of taking the next big step!"

I couldn't deny he was right. I could feel the change. People in the industry no longer considered No Pudge! to be just another tiny, home-based start-up. We were being taken seriously as a credible organization with a solid future.

I trusted him, so I tried to be patient and listen with an open mind, but *I don't want to do this anymore!* played like a broken record in my head, making it hard to focus.

"The first thing we need to do is find someone to run the day-to-day operation for you, and I have just the person. Then we'll get you out of the house and into a real office where you can work together as a team." He paused to take a breath. "Finally, I'll help you raise enough money to hire additional people and introduce new products."

I should have been thrilled. Here was a brilliant, business-savvy guy telling me my company was doing too well to sell and offering to walk me through the process of taking it to the next level. But I wasn't thrilled, I was drained. Mentally, physically, emotionally.

"I'm not trying to pressure you," he said. "If we bring someone else in, you can be as involved as you want. You just won't be bogged down by the day-to-day baloney."

When I talked to Sallie about Steve's idea, she said exactly what I thought she would — she wanted to help take No Pudge! to the next level and would do whatever she could to make this work.

For the next few weeks I tried to convince myself that Steve's route was the best one for both me and No

Pudge!. I met with the guy Steve thought would be perfect and liked him immensely. He had amazing experience and I knew that if I worked with him for the next three to five years we could get sales to $10 million — or more. It was a course of action that made complete business sense.

One small problem. . . I didn't want to. No Pudge! was the sun my life had revolved around for over eight long years. Twenty-four/seven, 365, I ate, drank, dreamt about, and lived No Pudge!. The boulder was getting bigger and the hill steeper, and I was tired of the unending struggle to keep inching it forward.

I didn't need to run a big company. I didn't want to run a big company. I wanted to be done.

Rather than have an honest conversation with Steve and Sallie, I simply dropped the ball. As spring rolled into summer, I pushed the topic of selling into the background and stopped discussing the long-term future of No Pudge!. In their seemingly limitless patience and understanding, they let it go. Traveling, trade shows, and running the day-to-day operation of a three-woman company experiencing double-digit growth kept me busy enough. Besides, it was easier *not* to think about it. Thinking about it would eventually require action, and right now, inaction was the preferred path of least resistance.

Then, a week before A.J. was leaving for his freshman year of college, he landed a sucker punch that brought my carefully orchestrated avoidance to a grinding halt.

The year before, Paul and I had decided that someday we'd like to live in the small town where his brother lived. We weren't ready to buy, but we connected with a local realtor who could keep an eye open just in case the "perfect" lot came on the market.

The week before, the realtor had e-mailed an interesting listing, and when Saturday dawned warm and sunny, we decided to drive over, take a look, and then land at Dick and Linda's for a swim and dinner. Already starting to feel the separation anxiety, I asked A.J. to come along. He good-naturedly agreed.

"If there's a view here, I sure don't see it." I grumbled as I carefully stepped over trees stumps and rocks hidden by layers of fallen leaves. Through the dense trees, Paul and the realtor were barely visible. Stopping at a tree marked with an orange ribbon, I turned to A.J.

He looked back towards the road, as if assuring himself his father was out of earshot. "Mom, what are you doing?"

I gestured towards the marked tree. "Trying to figure out where we are on the lot."

"No, Mom. That's not what I mean." His tone was that of a patient adult speaking to a not-too-bright child. "I thought you were going to sell the Pig."

"I am. One of these days. I'm just not sure if it's the right time. . . ." My voice trailed off.

"What are you thinking?" His tone of voice and the look of intense frustration in his dark brown eyes caught me totally off guard.

Whoa! What's going on here? I was completely blindsided by what followed.

"What's it gonna take? You had your heart thing, you don't know how long it's gonna be before Dad needs chemo, and you have no idea how long he has left. It's time."

I stared at him.

He wasn't done. "You work ridiculous hours, you travel all the time. This is stupid. Sell the Pig. Now. You're wasting time you don't have."

Out of the mouths of babes. . .

Chapter 40

A.J.'s reality check hit me like a bucket of ice water. Instead of taking a good, hard look at my priorities after Paul's diagnosis, I'd pushed my family and myself back to normal at warp speed. When, only weeks later, I got slammed with my own bona fide kick in the ass, I still didn't stop to think that maybe working 24/7 wasn't the best use of a life. It took my seventeen-year-old son to force me to face the fact I was on the wrong road.

"You're right," I said to A.J. "I'll call Steve on Monday."

He nodded. "Good." The conversation ended as abruptly as it began. I was his mom. He believed if I told him I would do something, I would do it.

"A.J.'s right," Steve said when I told him. "It's time. Let's do this."

On September 1, 2003, we signed a contract and made it official: No Pudge! Foods, Incorporated was for sale.

"This won't be quick or easy," Steve warned me. "You're in for a rollercoaster ride that's going to be more down than up."

I shrugged off his words. This was No Pudge!. We had a delicious, unique product line, a devoted costumer following, and we were experiencing double-digit growth. What more could people need?

Well, to start — a better gross margin, lower manufacturing costs, sales of $5 million or more, and, oh yeah — about that double-digit growth. . .

The "Atkins Revolution" was on its way to breaking the sound barrier and suddenly everyone was asking: "Are these brownies low-carb?"

Ah. . . No.

At the winter trade shows, every third booth seemed to feature low-carb something-or-other. Sallie and I blithely reassured ourselves that this carb-cutting insanity was a "flash in the pan." But when low-carb was practically the theme of the summer shows and sales started to slip, we began singing a different tune.

"Why *now*?" I groaned to Steve daily.

I imagined he'd been sitting in his quiet home office, glancing at the clock, knowing that every passing minute brought him closer to dealing with a near-hysterical female. He handled me much the same way he dealt with his Maltese pup, Karma, who erupted into a barking frenzy at any noise.

"We'll get this done." Calm, even tone. "We're doing all we can." Patient and soothing. "Just keep running the company as if you have no intention of selling it, and I'll do the rest." Reassuring and in charge.

I kept my nose to the grindstone, but it wasn't easy.

In mid-May, Sallie and I found ourselves in blistering-hot North Carolina for the Haddon House show. We were going through our usual, last-minute, "are we ready?" routine in the hotel ballroom when Ray, one of the company reps on the trade show circuit, wandered over. We managed to carry on an amiable conversation as we hustled around the booth. Finally, with a casual "Have a good show," he turned to leave, and then, as an afterthought, turned back.

"Listen, if you ever think about selling your company, let me know."

Sallie and I froze. *Huh? What'd he say?* We looked first at each other, then back at him.

"Reily is always on the lookout for good, small companies to acquire." He reached out for a brownie sample. "I think they'd love No Pudge!," he concluded before dropping the morsel into his mouth.

I was on the phone to Steve the first minute I could get away. "He thinks they'd love us!"

"I've never heard of them," he admitted. "And I'm busy all day with another project."

You mean holding my hand isn't your primary focus? Ah, c'mon!

"But I'll see what I can find out about them, first thing in the morning."

Steve is the research king. If there's information out there, he'll find it. He learned that Reily Foods was a multimillion dollar company still owned by the same New Orleans family that founded it over a hundred years ago. And miracle of miracles, when he called Ray's contact a few days later, it turned out that Ray was right. They *were* interested in No Pudge!

Six weeks later, after several phone calls with Reily and a couple of face-to-face meetings, Steve decided the time had come to take the next step. "Don't get too excited," he cautioned me, "but I think there's a reasonable chance these guys may be your buyer. It's time to call Connie."

He was referring to the other half of my Let's Make a Deal dream team: my lawyer, Connie Rakowsky.

Whenever I called Connie, I pictured her in her elegant office, looking out her big windows at the New Hampshire state house's gold dome. Impeccably dressed in a dark suit, she answers the phone and then leans forward, chin-length bob swinging slightly, and hits a timer that sets the billable hour dial spinning. Thank God she'd lowered her rates for me when we first met; it was the only way I could afford to have her — as she put it — watch my back, front, and both sides.

"Steve says it's time," I told her.

"Congratulations." Her voice was quiet and steady. "You ready for this? It could get crazy."

"So I hear. And I should warn you: we're dealing exclusively with Southern men."

"Sounds like fun," she laughed. "I can handle them."

I didn't doubt it for a second. I pitied the poor soul who underestimated either her gender or her calm demeanor. She is, in fact, a brilliant bulldog.

"I've seen a lot of deals fall apart once negotiations get serious, so don't get your hopes up."

"Funny, Steve keeps saying the exact same thing," I told her. "Don't worry, I won't."

Baloney. Paul and I were now empty-nesters, and the topic of our nightly after-dinner-glass-of-wine conversation was almost exclusively what we'd do "when." We began to believe this was *it.*

Big mistake. The rollercoaster ride was about to go into overdrive. . . .

As suddenly as Reily had appeared, they disappeared.

"I've left several messages and a couple of e-mails for George and I haven't heard a word," had been Steve's daily report for two weeks.

"Look," he said one night as the air conditioner worked overtime to keep my under-the-eaves office tolerable. "I think it's time to put the Reily folder away and move on."

I felt like throwing up.

"This is the way it goes sometimes," he said. "They've probably found something else."

I could tell from his tone of voice that I wasn't the only one upset.

"What am I supposed to do now?" I wailed.

"What you've been doing for the last ten years," he replied calmly. "Run your company."

It took every ounce of restraint I had to keep from throwing myself on the floor in a full blown toddler tantrum, screaming, "*I don't wanna!*"

Then out of the blue in late September, Reily popped back up and proclaimed they were ready to negotiate in earnest.

Having learned absolutely nothing, my "hope-meter" immediately whipped into overdrive. Even Steve was encouraged. During our first post-reappearance conference call with Connie, he told us, "I think they're ready to move forward quickly."

"Great," Connie said. "Let's wrap this sucker up."

There's a bad joke buried in here somewhere. . . . What do you get when an anxious entrepreneur, a Jewish consultant from New Jersey, and a female attorney from New Hampshire try to push a car full of Southern male senior executives down the road? Gridlock.

In mid-November we were still shlogging through a sea of minutiae. I was spending so much time at Connie's office that I no longer had to be "announced." I'd wave to the receptionist in the fancy lobby that had once intimidated me and off I'd go, stopping in the employee kitchen for a cup of coffee on the way.

Day after day, Connie and I planted ourselves at the large mahogany table in her conference room. The speaker phone situated between us would begin to crackle, and Steve's disembodied voice filled the air. "I'm on," he'd announce. Then more static, until finally voices direct from The Big Easy would blast into the room. We never knew who — or how many — senior executives would be on any call. They would identify themselves and off we'd go.

I cannot for the life of me remember any of the particulars that came up during those calls. What I can remember is sitting through hours and hours of often tense conversation while Connie, Steve, and the Reily power-dudes hashed out what I thought were ridiculous, obvious, and painfully boring details. Connie would roll her eyes or throw up her hands, and then calmly explain to the voice in the speaker why what they were asking for simply wasn't going to work.

I obediently kept my mouth shut, trying not to visualize Connie's hourly rate–meter spinning like a top. "Maybe I could start cleaning the bathrooms around here to work off my bill," I told her.

She didn't look up from the yellow, legal pad where she was intent on scribbling notes from our latest marathon session. "Yeah, sorry about that."

"You're supposed to tell me it isn't going to be that bad."

She stopped scribbling and looked at me. "You want me to lie?"

I dropped my head onto the conference table and groaned. "This damn thing better close." I raised my head and smiled sweetly. "Or we're both in big trouble."

She laughed, then her expression turned serious. Putting down her pen, she swiveled the brown leather chair to face me. "I have to admit I've never seen a negotiation of this magnitude for a company of this size. If I'd known it was going to be this complicated," she patted the bulging file next to her, "I would have gotten an associate involved and saved you some money."

I shrugged. "Nothing we can do about that now. Besides," I grinned, "look at all the fun you'd be missing!"

No matter how or where I spent my day, it would end with me collapsed at my desk in New Hampshire, recapping the day with Steve at his desk in New Jersey.

"I don't believe these guys!" I'd rant. "This is taking for bloody ever!" Then I'd make the *big* mistake of complaining, "I can't get motivated to deal with the day-to-day details of No Pudge! anymore." Before this sentiment was even out of my mouth, Steve would smack me with a reality check: No one would want to buy a company that wasn't moving forward. Until we had a signed contract, and not one second before, my job was to run this company.

I wanted to gag.

On a cold, gray day just before Christmas, Sallie and I settled ourselves at my kitchen table to figure out our final numbers for the year. We'd sold over a quarter of a million cases of brownie mix, but it wasn't good enough. We spent hours trying to put a positive spin on the fact we were finishing the year with single-digit growth for the first time in the company's history. By midafternoon we were fried. Finally, Sallie tossed her pencil in the air and threw up her hands. "Hey, we're still in business," she announced. "That's a lot more than most small, carb-loaded companies can say."

"Great," I grumbled, searching for my glasses case, which had disappeared beneath mountains of scattered papers. "That should boost the price up a good million or two. . . ." I pulled the case from its papery grave, shoved my readers in, and glumly surveyed the chaos. "Is it too early to start drinking?"

Straight-faced, Sallie looked at her watch. "It's five o'clock somewhere."

We all assumed the New Orleans crew would want this wrapped up by the end of the year, but noooo. . . .

Thanksgiving passed, then Christmas, finally New Year's rolled by and the gentlemen from Reily moved with about as much speed as an old hound dog on a summer day in the bayou. The little No Pudge! team trudged into the New Year tired, stressed, and wanting to get this over with already! Then a light appeared at the end of the tunnel that, for once, didn't appear to be the headlight of an oncoming train.

I was on my way home from the grocery store in the late-afternoon dusk when my cell phone rang.

"I just had a call from George," Steve said instead of "Hello."

I immediately went on high alert. "They've changed their minds and want to forget the whole thing?"

"No. Don't drive off the road, but they want to announce they've bought No Pudge! at the Fancy Food Show."

I began to tingle. "*This* Fancy Food Show?" I asked him. "The one in three weeks?"

"Yup."

"You're sure they don't mean the one in New York in June?" I realized I'd just driven past my street.

"George specifically said 'San Francisco.'"

"*Woo hoo!*"

When I stopped yelling he said, "There's one small hitch."

I knew it. They've dropped their offer by 90 percent and want me to work for them for the rest of my life.

"They want you and Sallie to set up and run the booth at the show while their marketing people watch and learn."

That's it? "Sure! Absolutely! Whatever!" We had a date! A bona fide deadline to work towards.

"So we have to close by January 20 at the absolute latest," Steve finished.

January 20, here we come!

I leaned back in my desk chair and closed my burning eyes. The last few days had been ludicrously long and outrageously stressful. Today Connie, Steve, and I had spent the entire day — and evening — on the phone. It was now 10 p.m. on January 19. We were running out of time.

Footsteps came into the room. "Anything new?" Paul asked quietly.

I opened my eyes. "Connie just called to say she was done for the day and going home. Any more changes will have to wait until morning."

He perched on the edge of my desk, picked up a paperclip, and started twisting it out of shape. "Do you think it'll get done?"

"Honestly? I'm not sure." I gently took the bent wire from him and tossed it in the wastebasket. "Connie, Steve, and I talked about it and agreed that if it doesn't happen tomorrow, it ain't happenin'."

The twentieth dawned bright and cold.

Bundled against the freezing temperatures and lugging an overstuffed briefcase, I stood by the door and looked up at Paul. Under the overnight stubble, his cheeks were pale and he had circles under his eyes. His face reflected the worry and fatigue I felt. Leaning over, he gave me a kiss. "Good luck today," he said.

"Thanks. Keep your fingers crossed."

Driving to Connie's office, I tried to imagine how I'd feel if this sale slipped away and I came home empty-handed. I couldn't even go there — it was too scary. I didn't know if I had it in me to start over.

"More changes." Connie's lips were set in a thin line. She held up a pile of papers, then unceremoniously dropped them onto the conference-room table. "I'm not sure we're gonna be able to get this done today."

"Wonderful!" I dropped my briefcase on the floor and started peeling off wintry layers. "Really, why would I want this to close? Then I'd miss the joys of business travel," I said, throwing the coat on a chair. "The fun of balancing the books." I tossed my scarf and gloves on top of the coat. "The pure pleasure of standing in trade show booths for hours on end being polite to people who only want carb-less crap!" And with that I plopped into the leather chair next to her.

Laughing, she stood and reached for her empty mug. "Coffee?"

"No thanks. Think I'm wired enough."

We called Steve, then the three of us dialed into our scheduled call with Reily. Every change meant a reprint of every page, and the day dragged on. When we broke for lunch, I couldn't swallow the tuna on wheat but did manage to inhale every last potato chip crumb from my bag and Connie's. A half hour later we were back on the phone.

"Okay," a deep Southern drawl came through the speaker phone. "Guess that's it. We're ready to sign if you are."

Connie raised her eyebrows at me. When I nodded, she leaned towards the speaker. "Let's do it," she said firmly.

Steve's job was officially done, so he thanked everyone and signed off, knowing I'd call him as soon as it was over.

Connie started putting papers in front of me and, on autopilot, I signed. I felt like I was watching a movie — I couldn't grasp the reality of what was happening.

In another conference room, not far from the French Quarter, our slow-as-molasses Southern gentlemen had finally reached the finish line and were doing the same thing I was. Pages were signed and faxed. Faxes were received and acknowledged.

Just before five, Connie's paralegal came into the room, handed her a piece of paper and quietly left.

Connie looked at it then extended it to me. "The funds have been wired," she said. "It's done."

Dazed, I stared at the paper in my hand. Numbers totaling an amount of money I had only dreamt about stared back at me. Enough to finish paying for the boys' college educations, enough to build a new house if we wanted, enough, I hoped, for Paul to stop worrying about money. *I did it.* . . I had a momentary flash of standing in the farmhouse kitchen, the fudgy sweetness of a brownie made with yogurt melting across my tongue and the glimmer of a whatif growing in my brain.

"Congratulations." Connie reached across the space between us and squeezed my hand.

"Thanks." *Where's the elation?*

We started gathering papers. "When do you head to San Francisco?" she asked.

"Tomorrow morning. I have to be out of the house by 4:30 for a 7:30 flight."

Connie nodded. She looked drained. I wasn't the only one who'd been steamrollered by the stress of the past few days.

"Thanks for being here for me." I gave her a hug.

"Wouldn't have missed it. It was quite the experience." She patted my back. Then she handed me my coat. "Now get out of here, that husband of yours is waiting!"

I drove home through the rush-hour traffic, my brain in a fog. The effort of holding on through the long, wild ride had left me almost too wiped to comprehend it was over. All I wanted to do was go home, hug my husband, down a bottle of champagne, and sleep for a week.

When I walked in the house, Paul enveloped me in a bear hug. I nuzzled into his warm neck and inhaled the lingering, fresh scent of his favorite aftershave. *Home.*

"I am so proud of you," he said softly.

"Thanks." I pulled away and once again started stripping off layers. "I've gotta go up to the office and start getting stuff together for my trip."

"You go ahead," he said as he took my coat. "I was going to take you out for dinner but figured you'd be too tired, so I planned a nice dinner for here."

Bless you.

"I even bought a really good bottle of champagne."

I saw the pride mingled with concern in his brown eyes and offered a silent *Thank you* to the heavens. The strength of our commitment to each other, and a willingness to finally accept that we both had attitudes in need of adjustment, had enabled us to toss our 800-pound gorilla into the cold. I hoped whoever that gorilla was shacked up with now would be as lucky.

"The dinner part sounds wonderful, but can we save the champagne for when I get back? I've gotta get up at 3:45 tomorrow morning. . . ." *It's over. And I'm too tired for a glass of champagne. I didn't think it would be like this.*

"Absolutely. Go finish what you need to do, and I'll start dinner."

I leaned my forehead against the cold window of the 757 and stared at the monochromatic blue sky. In the seat next to me, Sallie was out like a light. Leaning back, I adjusted the tiny airline pillow.

Ten years. . . Amazing. . .

When I started No Pudge! I began a journey I could not, in my wildest dreams, have envisioned. Now I was about to start a new journey. I was equally clueless about life as an unemployed, fifty-five-year-old empty-nester. When I got back from San Francisco there'd be no stressful, demanding job, no kids to cater to — just a husband and a dog and endless possibilities. I felt the tiniest quiver of excitement.

My eyelids felt luxuriously heavy. I took a long breath and slowly let it out as the deep sleep of a worry-free mind enveloped me.

Epilogue

I have two vivid memories from that 2005 San Francisco Fancy Food Show. First, our 10' x 10' booth became "Reily Central." Senior executives had flown in from New Orleans, and I don't know whether they thought it was their responsibility to hang out at the booth, or they were just being friendly, or maybe it was that Sallie and I were so delightful, but they just couldn't drag themselves away. Whatever the reason, we found ourselves tripping over men in suits and assorted coats, bags, and briefcases left in the booth for "safekeeping." None of these guys seemed interested in actually working, so Sallie and I did our best to keep sample plates filled and to talk with customers while trying not to crash into one executive or another. Finally, Sallie had had enough.

"That's it," my five-foot-tall sidekick announced. "Out! All of you, out of here now. We can't get any work done with you hanging around." The suits scattered like startled crows. Once they cleared the area we looked at each other and laughed until we cried. The best part? Sallie had agreed to work for Reily to help guarantee a smooth transition, and she had just thrown the president of a multi-million dollar company—who happened to be her new boss—out of the booth.

My second memory wasn't so funny. Coming back from a bathroom break, I ran into a friend. The first words out of his mouth were, "Have you been sick? You look exhausted."

You mean I don't look like I'm celebrating? I told him my news, he congratulated me, and I continued on my way. All I could think was, *Screw the champagne and balloons—just give me a week's worth of zzzz's.*

When the show closed, Sallie and I packed up the booth to ship home. Kneeling beside one of the cartons, I slapped on an address label. The impact rocked me back on my heels. "Home" was Reily Foods, not No Pudge!. New Orleans, not New Hampshire. I heard another label hit cardboard.

"This doesn't feel right somehow," Sallie muttered.

We finished labeling in silence.

That night we celebrated our last business trip together at our favorite little Italian restaurant on Russian Hill. After toasting each other with "big girl drinks," we had an amazing meal. And then we charged it to Reily.

A few months later, Connie and I met for one of our regular I-miss-seeing-you-all-the-time lunches. I wound into gripe-mode almost before her navy-suited fanny hit the chair.

"How many times did Reily tell me," I dropped my voice an octave and added a thick Southern accent. "'Lindsay,'" I mimicked. "'Your continued involvement in No Pudge! is critically important.'" The drawl disappeared and, trying not to make a scene in the small, crowded restaurant, I leaned across the table until we were almost nose-to-nose. "You were there! You heard them!"

She looked calmly down at her menu. "What are you having?"

"Steve keeps telling me this always happens when a big company buys a little one," I grumbled. "But they just fired two of our best brokers! And they haven't updated the website once! They're gonna lose. . ."

"Lindsay!" Connie's eyes zeroed in on me like lasers. "The check cleared," she said in her no-nonsense, lawyer voice. "Move on."

Her words had the same effect as A.J.'s "Sell the Pig" speech two years earlier—a reality check that hit like a bucket of ice water. "You know," I said, feeling slightly dazed and a hundred pounds lighter. "You're right."

A couple of months later, Paul and I moved into a new house and I poured myself into getting settled. When there was no more "settling" to do, I found myself flailing—looking for projects. Then one gorgeous mid-July afternoon, I grabbed a book and planted myself on the porch glider. My eyes grew heavy, and I moved to the hammock strung between two shady oaks. It felt so good I repeated the entire scenario the next day. The transition from nonstop crazy woman to guilt-free lady of leisure had finally begun.

"Guess what?" Tanned and smiling, Paul walked in the door one afternoon after a five-day bicycle trip in Arizona, and dropped his suitcase on the floor. "I've made a decision!"

It was four years after my comeuppance lunch with Connie. After a rocky course of chemo two years earlier, Paul was in full remission, feeling great and working half-time. For the first time since college, he had the flexibility to "play" during the week.

"You don't even say hello?" I teased as I stood on tiptoes and wrapped my arms around his neck. "How about—'Oh honey, I missed you *so* much'?"

"Yeah, yeah, whatever," he laughed. "I have something to tell you." He stood there beaming. "I've decided it's time to retire!"

This was something we'd been talking about for ages, but even after twenty years, the bankruptcy and subsequent financial worries still haunted him, and he'd been too cautious to commit. Now he grabbed me and started dancing around the back hall. "Life's too short and I'm ready to play," he sang.

That night we opened one of the bottles of wine we'd brought home from our family trip to Italy. We'd had much to celebrate then, too: the end of Paul's chemo, our twenty-fifth wedding anniversary, A.J.'s graduation from college, and the fact that both boys had landed great jobs in New York City—exactly where they wanted to be. I raised the glass of deep red Montepulciano. "To retirement, to wonderful adventures, and . . . to us."

He solemnly touched his glass to mine. "We've earned this." He took a long swallow of the wine then leaned forward to kiss me. "I love you."

"I love you, too." I leaned back in my chair. "Now, on to serious matters. Where're we going first?"

I was cleaning up the breakfast dishes the next morning when Paul walked in. "We need to talk." The dark tan from his days in the sun couldn't mask the gray pallor of his face. The pain in his eyes hit me like a sucker punch.

"What's wrong?" I was finding it hard to breathe.

He stood there mute, staring at me and shaking his head slowly.

"Oh God, Frooch, what is it?" The boys. Something had happened to one of the boys.

Then he told me. Scott, the man who handled all of our investment money, had locked his doors and disappeared. Every penny, including the money from the sale of No Pudge!, was gone.

It was the income from that money on which we had built all our retirement dreams.

As I write this, a year has passed since that day. Our investment guy pleaded guilty to fraud and was sentenced to fifteen years in prison. The lawyers have told us that all the money is gone and not to expect restitution. So Paul is back to working full-time and away a lot, and our house is on the market. When it sells, we'll move to New York to be closer to our boys.

As you can imagine, the experience of losing everything—again—has been devastating. But it has also been enlightening. I began No Pudge! to make lots of money so that my husband would stop worrying. But early in the No Pudge! journey, it became about so much more. Thanks to my smiling pink Pig, I discovered parts of me I never knew existed, surprising myself constantly with my audacity and courage, and often wondering, Who is this confident, intelligent woman and where did *I* go? I don't wonder that anymore.

Freedom from financial worry is a legitimate goal, but I've learned that self-respect, a loving support system, and a healthy, close-knit family are truly the most important things in life. A greedy criminal might find a way to steal our money, but he can never steal the woman I became by putting on an apron with a cute piggy on the front, baking some damn good brownies, and taking on the world.

Author's Note

I need your help.

In the fall of 2010, after several months of trying – and failing - to get the attention of a literary agent, I decided to self-publish this memoir. What that means is no publisher will be writing nice, fat checks for promotion or advertising and there is no distribution channel for moving the book into mainstream stores. I am totally dependent on readers like you passing the word to other readers and hoping that, like with No Pudge!, the word will spread.

So, I have a favor to ask. If you liked *The Pig and Me* (and I hope you loved it!), please tell your family, friends and fellow book club members about it – or better yet, buy them a copy! They will thank you – and you know I will!

Warmly,
Lindsay

The Pig and Me is available in select independent bookstores and on Amazon.com in either print or ebook formats.

Acknowledgements

I turned to my very smart and talented oldest son, Adam, for first readings and guidance. His “It’s great Mom, but why don’t you try putting some of this into scene and adding some dialogue?” pushed me to take the first step from essay to book.

When I got bogged down early on and threatened to quit, Steve Mintz made me promise to talk to Suzanne Kingsbury first. Bless you Steve. Suzanne is a teacher/editor extraordinaire and I feel like I received the gift of a one-on-one course in Creative Writing. I cannot begin to describe how much I learned from Suzanne. Without her patient teaching and guidance, there would not have been a book for you to read.

Ah, the Breakfast Babes… Eloise Adams, Janet Crowder, Gerry DeGeorge, Ellen Eisenhower, Diane Essex, Pat Greenberg, Janet Millay, Mary O’Brien, and Donna Solod. For the past three years, rain, snow or beautiful sunshine, this group has gathered almost every morning to share coffee, friendship, support and loads of laughter. Some were early readers; all were cheerleaders. Thanks Girls.

I have to thank my friend Sallie Bowling, for having the patience to read every damn version, the courage to be an honest critic, and the ability to remember details I thought were gone forever.

Finally, how do you acknowledge the three men who are the loves of your life? I guess you just say *Thank You* and know that they know…

Thank you Adam, AJ & Frooch. For everything.